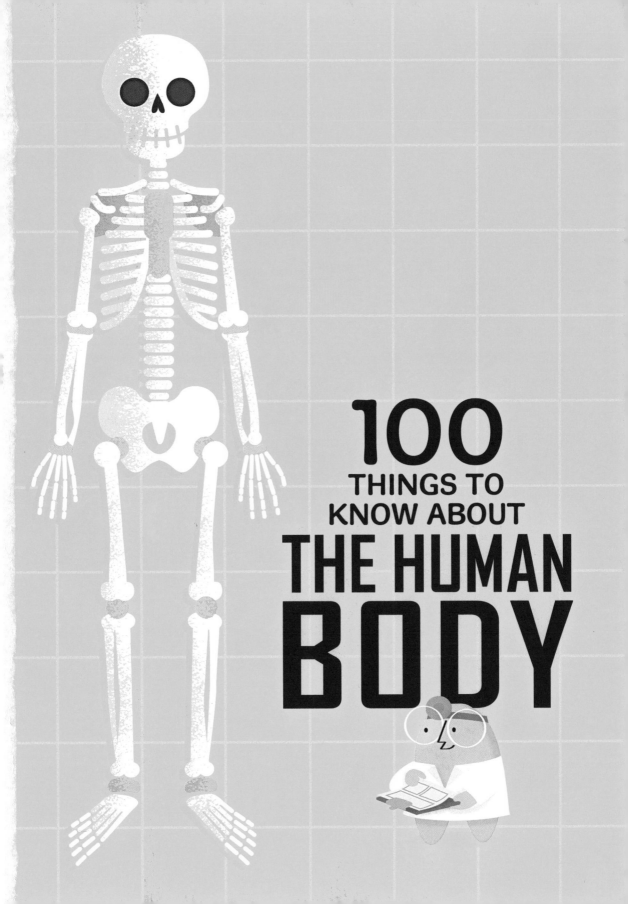

100
THINGS TO
KNOW ABOUT
THE HUMAN
BODY

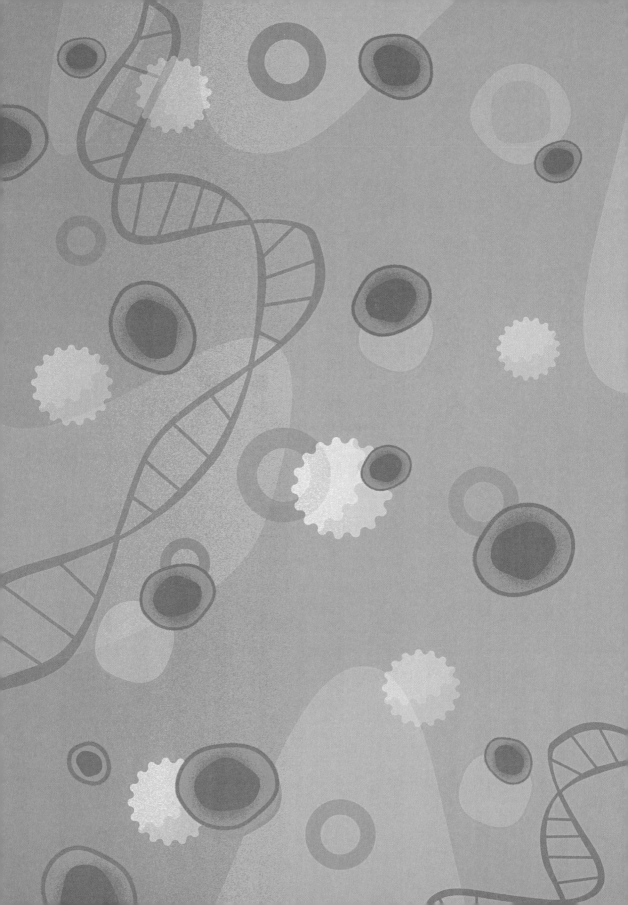

100
THINGS TO
KNOW ABOUT
THE HUMAN
BODY

Written by
Alex Frith, Minna Lacey,
Jonathan Melmoth & Matthew Oldham

Illustrated by
Federico Mariani & Danny Schlitz

Layout and design
Matthew Bromley, Freya Harrison,
Lenka Hrehova & Vickie Robinson

Human body expert
Dr. Kristina Routh

1 You'll sleep for 23 years...
in your lifetime.

And you'll walk – or roll – the equivalent of **3 times** around the Earth.

Your heart will beat **2,500,000,000** (2.5 billion) times. That's 100,000 times every day.

Your lungs will take **650 million** breaths.

You'll dream over **100,000** dreams.

Your hair will grow **590 miles** – the distance from Paris to London and back again.

6ft, 6in of hair will grow out of your nose...

...and your nails will grow **8ft, 2in**.

You'll use the toilet **155,490** times.

That's 6 times a day, 42 times a week and... oh, I'd better go.

Saliva

You'll produce enough saliva to fill up a fuel tanker.

You'll need to drink about **16,000 gallons** of water to stay alive.

You'll shed over **100lbs** of skin. That's the weight of a large dog.

These facts are based on the current worldwide average lifespan: **71 years**. But scientists think that some children alive today may live as long as **150 years** – which means their bodies will have done a whole lot more by the time they die.

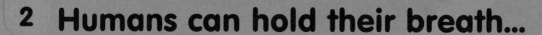

2 Humans can hold their breath...

for as long as 20 minutes.

Most adults can only hold their breath for 30 seconds to 1 minute.
But freedivers – swimmers who go underwater without a snorkel or
aqualungs – can train their bodies to last 20 times longer without breathing.

Before a dive, freedivers practice
relaxing their bodies completely. This
makes them need less oxygen and
slows their heartbeat.

Freedivers learn how to
resist a powerful urge to
breathe out carbon dioxide
and take in oxygen.

3 The blink of an eye...

is not as fast as you might think.

The average blink of an eye lasts for just a third of a second. But your eyelids don't actually move very quickly – only around 0.5mph, just twice the speed of a walking tortoise. Here are some other body speeds:

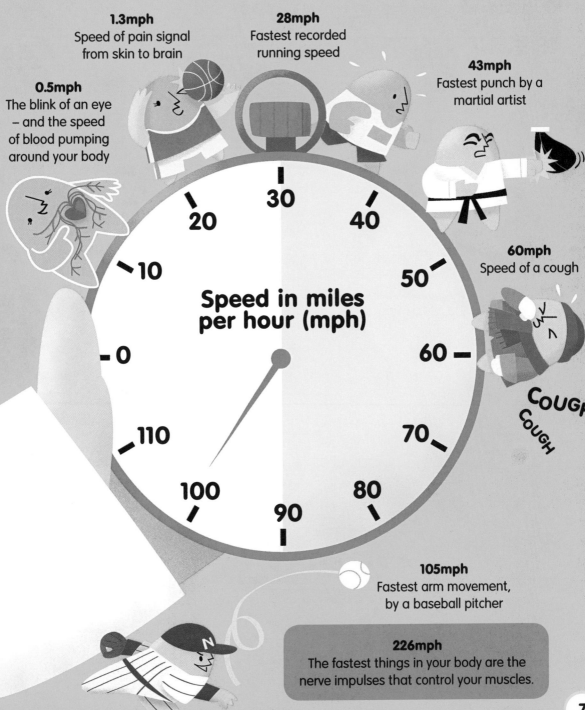

1.3mph
Speed of pain signal
from skin to brain

28mph
Fastest recorded
running speed

43mph
Fastest punch by a
martial artist

0.5mph
The blink of an eye
– and the speed
of blood pumping
around your body

60mph
Speed of a cough

Speed in miles
per hour (mph)

20 30 40
10 50
0 60
110 70
100 80
90

COUGH
COUGH

105mph
Fastest arm movement,
by a baseball pitcher

226mph
The fastest things in your body are the
nerve impulses that control your muscles.

Your body is a network...

of ten life-support systems.

Find out what **cells**, **hormones** and other body words mean on pages 120-121.

ENDOCRINE SYSTEM

One way your organs tell each other what to do is by using chemical messengers called **hormones**. These are made in parts called **glands**, known together as the endocrine system.

RESPIRATORY SYSTEM

Your **lungs** *respire*, or breathe, which means they get fresh oxygen into your blood system, and get rid of waste gases.

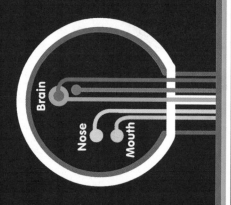

Brain

Nose

Mouth

Lung

Heart

Spleen

Stomach

Pancreas

Liver

Intestines

Gland

Kidney

NERVOUS SYSTEM

Your **brain**, the organ that controls most other systems, relays messages to the rest of your body through a network of **nerve cells**.

CARDIOVASCULAR SYSTEM

A series of **blood vessels** carry blood all around your body, pumped by your **heart**. Among other things, blood carries **oxygen**, a chemical all your organs need to work.

DIGESTIVE SYSTEM

Your body needs food to grow and repair itself. Your **stomach, intestines** and other digestive organs break down – or *digest* – food, absorbing **nutrients** from it and removing unwanted waste.

IMMUNE SYSTEM

Your immune system is made up of organs, tissues and a network of parts called **lymph vessels** that help to protect your body against disease.

URINARY SYSTEM

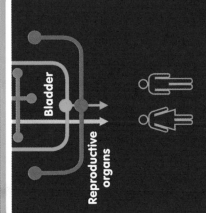

Bladder

Reproductive organs

Your body needs to clean waste and even poisons out of your blood. This starts in your **kidneys,** that help create waste fluid called **urine.**

REPRODUCTIVE SYSTEM

The organs of the body which allow adults to create and grow a **new baby.**

SKELETAL SYSTEM

Your **bones** make up your **skeleton,** which supports you, protects many organs, and helps you move.

MUSCULAR SYSTEM

Muscles move your bones, and also keep organs such as your heart and stomach working.

5 Your blood vessels cover...

over 60,000 miles (100,000km).

Blood flows all around your body, through a network of hollow tubes called **blood vessels**. There are three kinds: arteries, veins and capillaries.

Arteries carry blood full of oxygen from your heart and lungs to the rest of your body.

Capillaries

Veins carry blood from all parts of the body back to the heart and lungs.

Blood carries vital oxygen and energy from food to reach every part of your body.

Capillaries are the smallest blood vessels – thinner than a human hair. They link arteries to veins within your muscles and organs.

In reality, low-oxygen blood in your veins looks dark red.

High-oxygen blood in your arteries looks bright red.

If you placed all your blood vessels end-to-end, they would reach more than twice around the world.

6 Goosebumps...

are supposed to keep you warm and safe.

Goosebumps are an automatic reaction to being cold or afraid. They make the arms on your body stand up straight, and some experts think that, thousands of years ago, they helped extra-hairy humans stay safe.

How goosebumps work
A muscle at the base of each hair tenses, making it stand on end.

The skin around the hair forms a hard mound – a goosebump.

Ancient uses
Thuosands of years ago, humans had longer, thicker hair. Goosebumps helped in at least two ways:

①

Warming up
Hair standing on end traps air close to the skin.

This blanket of air helps the body to retain warmth.

②

Scaring off predators
Spiked-up hair makes things appear larger – and scarier.

It might have been enough to make a dangerous predator think twice before attacking.

These days, human hair is much thinner, so goosebumps hardly make a difference.

7 Your stomach would eat itself...

if it wasn't lined with mucus.

Mucus is a slimy substance found throughout the body. It lines the walls of the stomach, acting as a protective barrier against the strong acids your stomach produces to break down food.

Food pipe (Esophagus)

Mucus helps food slip down the food pipe.

The **snot** in your nose is another example of mucus.

Mucus is made of:

94% Water

5% Mucin (a gel made from proteins)

1% Other compounds

Your body produces up to **50oz** of mucus every day. That's enough to fill **7 glasses**.

STOMACH
Mucus is runny enough to cover every part of the stomach's bumpy **stomach wall**.

Stomach wall

TO SMALL INTESTINE

Stomach acid dissolves food – but it doesn't affect mucus, leaving the wall of the stomach protected.

Bumps in the stomach wall called **gastric folds**

Sometimes a hole forms in the mucus lining. Any acid that falls into the hole will eat away at the stomach wall, and can cause a wound called a **stomach ulcer**.

8 Your intestines can't digest food...

without the aid of millions of bacteria.

After leaving your stomach, food passes into your **small** and **large intestines**, where nutrients are absorbed. Inside are millions of tiny living creatures, mainly types of **bacteria** or **fungi**. Most of them help break down different types of food into substances that your body can absorb.

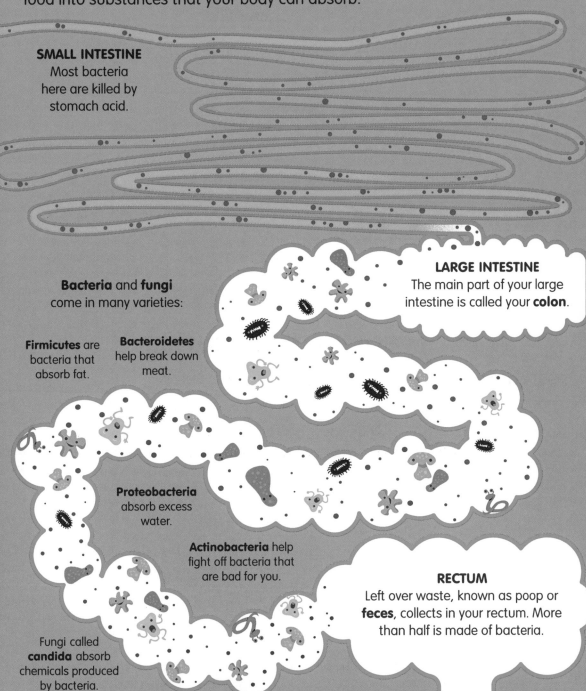

SMALL INTESTINE
Most bacteria here are killed by stomach acid.

Bacteria and **fungi** come in many varieties:

Firmicutes are bacteria that absorb fat.

Bacteroidetes help break down meat.

Proteobacteria absorb excess water.

Actinobacteria help fight off bacteria that are bad for you.

Fungi called **candida** absorb chemicals produced by bacteria.

LARGE INTESTINE
The main part of your large intestine is called your **colon**.

RECTUM
Left over waste, known as poop or **feces**, collects in your rectum. More than half is made of bacteria.

9 Ears get longer...

even after they've stopped growing.

Ears are mostly made of cartilage and skin, making them very flexible. But this flexibility also means that over a long period of time, their shape is gradually affected by gravity (the force that pulls everything downwards).

Young person
Cartilage and skin contain elastic fibers, that allow stretched ears to spring back into shape.

Old person
Over time, gravity stretches the fibers. Eventually, many of them break.

Your body stops growing by the age of 21, but your ears never stop getting longer. That's why old people often have **big ears**.

10 A five-year-old's mouth...

can hold up to 52 teeth at the same time.

Children grow up to 20 'milk' or 'baby' teeth between the ages of 0 and 5 – technically known as **deciduous teeth**. These are pushed out by a maximum of 32 'adult' or **permanent teeth** – making 52 teeth in total.

By age 5, most children have all their deciduous teeth in their mouth...

...while their permanent teeth are hiding inside the gums, waiting to come through.

11 Laughter is infectious...

and good for your health.

Just hearing the sound of laughter triggers the brain and makes you want to laugh back, which comes with many health benefits.

People rarely laugh just because they find something funny. Scientists believe it's an important part of speech and communication, showing agreement or understanding.

LAUGHTER

Burns up to **40 calories** in just **15 minutes**, by using around **43 different muscles**.

Increases **blood flow**, which helps keep the heart healthy and the brain alert.

Causes the body to produce extra **white blood cells**, which help to fight off infections.

Triggers the release of **endorphins**, hormones with powerful pain-numbing effects.

Reduces the levels of **cortisol** in the body, a hormone associated with **stress**.

Laughter is *great* medicine.

You're 30 times more likely to laugh with other people than alone.

12 Your body has a blueprint...

hidden inside your cells.

Your body is made up of billions of tiny parts called **cells**. Cells are designed to do different jobs, following instructions from a chemical they contain known as **DNA**. DNA in turn is made up of pairs of chemicals. Each pair is part of a code for building bodies.

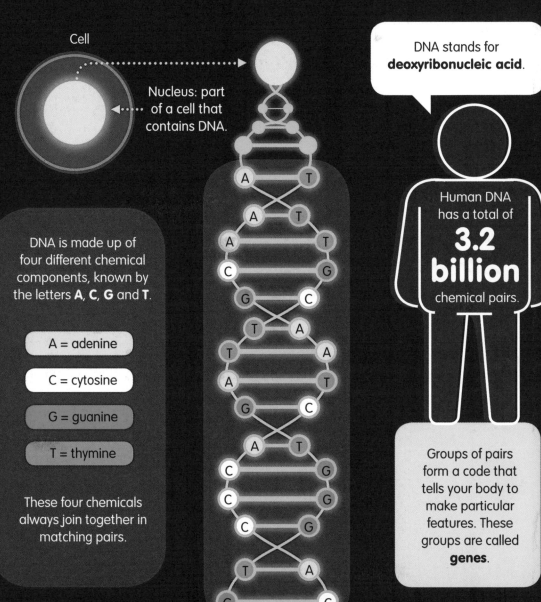

Cell

Nucleus: part of a cell that contains DNA.

DNA stands for **deoxyribonucleic acid**.

DNA is made up of four different chemical components, known by the letters **A**, **C**, **G** and **T**.

A = adenine

C = cytosine

G = guanine

T = thymine

These four chemicals always join together in matching pairs.

Human DNA has a total of

3.2 billion

chemical pairs.

Groups of pairs form a code that tells your body to make particular features. These groups are called **genes**.

So far, DNA experts have counted **22,000 genes** in the human body. But some think they might find many more.

13 Girls have more DNA...

than boys.

Boys and girls all have the same kind of DNA, except for one section. The section that makes boys be boys is much smaller than the equivalent part of a girl's DNA.

Inside a person's cells, DNA comes in 46 separate sections known as **chromosomes**. There are 22 identical pairs of chromosomes, each given a number, and a final pair, known by the letters X and Y, that are not always identical.

Cell nucleus from a girl's body

Cell nucleus from a boy's body

The only difference between boy and girl DNA is that girls have two copies of an X chromosome...

...while boys have just one X chromosome, and one Y chromosome.

Differences between the DNA in a Y and an X chromosome are the main reason why boys and girls develop different bodies.

Each X chromosome contains around **153 million pairs** of DNA material.

Y chromosomes are much smaller. Each contains around **59 million pairs** of DNA material.

14 Surgeons used to scan the sky...

before operating on their patients.

Until the 1700s, doctors in Europe consulted astronomical charts and calendars, before carrying out surgery. They believed different star signs controlled different parts of the body. If the Moon and stars weren't in the correct alignment, it was considered unsafe to operate.

Alongside the astronomical charts, doctors referred to diagrams such as this one, called a **zodiac man**, showing which star signs ruled different body parts.

ARIES	CANCER	LIBRA	CAPRICORN
Head, eyes	Chest	Kidneys	Knees, bones, skin
TAURUS	**LEO**	**SCORPIO**	**AQUARIUS**
Neck, throat, ears	Heart, spine, spleen	Reproductive organs, pelvis, bladder	Ankles
GEMINI	**VIRGO**	**SAGITTARIUS**	**PISCES**
Lungs, arms, fingers	Intestines, pancreas, gallbladder, liver	Thighs, legs	Feet

15 Flowers and trees...

can cure disease.

Many medicines used today are based on ancient herbal remedies. In labs, chemists have managed to identify and recreate the key chemicals in certain plants – including poisonous ones. These are made into medicines that can relieve or even cure all sorts of complaints.

Treats malaria

From Cinchona tree

QUININE

From foxgloves

Treats heart disease

Treats headaches

From willow tree

DIGITALIS

ASPIRIN

Treats lung disorders

From deadly nightshade

Treats memory loss

From snowdrops

TIOTROPIUM

GALANTAMINE

Treats leukaemia

From rosy periwinkle

Treats intense pain

From poppies

Treats forms of cancer

From pacific yew tree

VINCRISTINE

MORPHINE

PACLITAXEL

So far, chemists have studied **70,000** different plant species to look for medicines. There are at least **300,000** more to study...

16 You can't catch a cold...

by being out in the cold.

Some illnesses, known as **infectious diseases**, spread from person to person. Most are caused by germs – tiny creatures such as **bacteria** or **viruses**. But no infectious diseases are caused by being too hot or too cold.

Splutter!

Achoo!

Coughing and sneezing

Colds are caused by different viruses. The only way you can catch a cold is by being around someone who has a cold virus.

Touching and kissing

Sharing food and drink

It *is* possible to catch a disease from a *toilet seat*...

...but it's actually far less likely than catching one from a *door handle*.

Worrying about getting sick from a toilet seat is a little like worrying you're going to get struck by lightning.

Most germs need a body to host them, but some can survive outside a body. Here are some that can pass between people who touch the same things.

Your **skin** stops most germs from getting into your body. The best way to avoid spreading and catching germs is to **wash your hands**.

E. coli (bacteria)

Can cause diarrhea.

Streptococcus (bacteria)

Can cause a sore throat.

Norovirus

Can cause vomiting and diarrhea.

17 The world's deadliest disease...

is spread by a blood-sucking insect.

One disease has killed more people than any other in history – **malaria**. It's one of the oldest diseases on Earth, and has killed *billions*. But it's not always fatal. In fact, more than half the people who catch malaria survive.

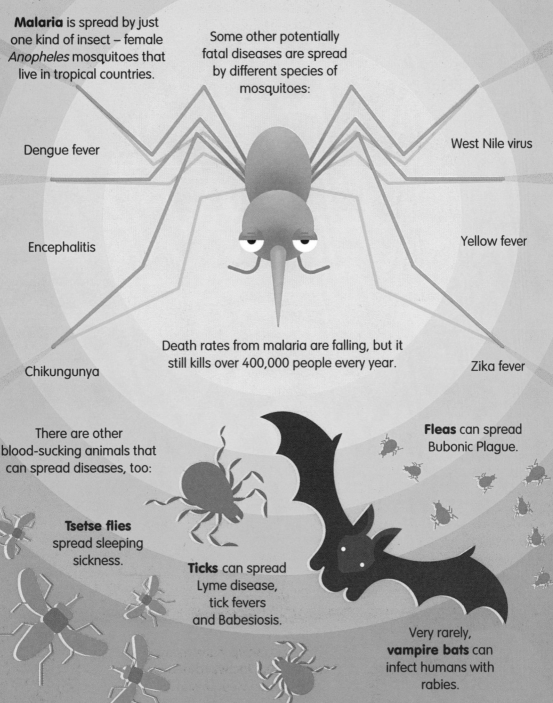

Malaria is spread by just one kind of insect – female *Anopheles* mosquitoes that live in tropical countries.

Some other potentially fatal diseases are spread by different species of mosquitoes:

Dengue fever

West Nile virus

Encephalitis

Yellow fever

Death rates from malaria are falling, but it still kills over 400,000 people every year.

Chikungunya

Zika fever

There are other blood-sucking animals that can spread diseases, too:

Fleas can spread Bubonic Plague.

Tsetse flies spread sleeping sickness.

Ticks can spread Lyme disease, tick fevers and Babesiosis.

Very rarely, **vampire bats** can infect humans with rabies.

You're taller in the morning...
than you are in the evening.

There are flexible discs in your spine that become thicker or thinner depending on your activity. They're thickest after you've been lying down, making you a little bit taller.

The bones in your spine are called **vertebrae**.

Between the vertebrae are rings called **intervertebral discs**. These contain a squashy gel that cushions impacts and allows the spine to move smoothly.

After a normal day

Most people spend the day standing, sitting upright and walking.

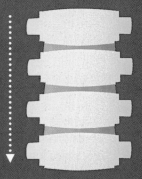

Gravity, the force that pulls everything down to the ground, presses the vertebrae together. This **squashes** the discs between them.

After a night's rest

Most people lie down in bed overnight.

Lying flat relieves the downward pressure on the discs and allows them to **expand** slowly into thick rings.

When you get up in the morning, you are up to **0.5 inches** taller than when you went to bed.

19 Your blood...

is made inside your bones.

Most of the cells in your blood only live for a few months, so your body needs to make a constant supply. Blood cells are created in **bone marrow** – a soft, spongy tissue that fills spaces inside some of your bones.

Red bone marrow, where blood cells are made

Inside your femur (thigh bone)

Yellow bone marrow contains mostly fat.

Red bone marrow creates a steady supply of undeveloped cells, called **stem cells**.

Each stem cell will grow into a particular type of blood cell.

Red blood cells help carry oxygen around your body, and carry carbon dioxide away.

White blood cells help the body fight infection.

Platelets help your blood clot, by sticking together, and forming a scab over a cut.

All these cells are carried in a watery liquid called **plasma**.

The new blood then enters your blood vessels to travel around your whole body.

20 Your body can tell the time...

even if you can't.

Lots of bodily processes follow a 24-hour cycle to help you make the best use of the daylight hours. The part of your brain that keeps time is called the **suprachiasmatic nucleus**, or body clock.

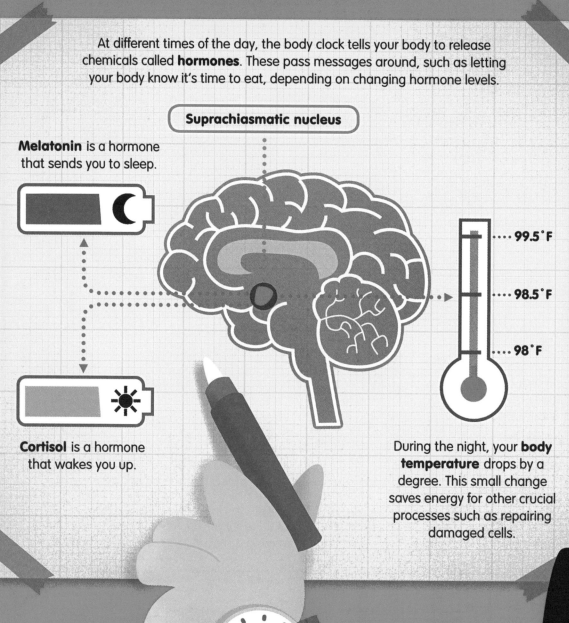

At different times of the day, the body clock tells your body to release chemicals called **hormones**. These pass messages around, such as letting your body know it's time to eat, depending on changing hormone levels.

Suprachiasmatic nucleus

Melatonin is a hormone that sends you to sleep.

99.5°F

98.5°F

98°F

Cortisol is a hormone that wakes you up.

During the night, your **body temperature** drops by a degree. This small change saves energy for other crucial processes such as repairing damaged cells.

This is how the body clock works for a typical adult:

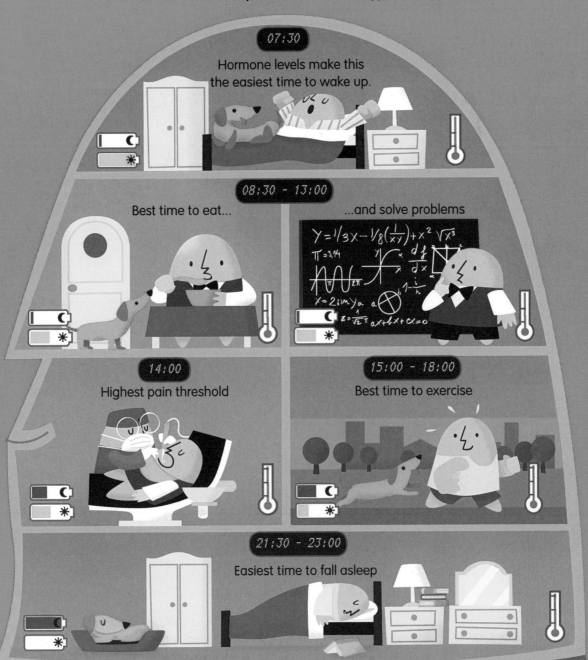

07:30

Hormone levels make this the easiest time to wake up.

08:30 - 13:00

Best time to eat...

...and solve problems

$$Y = \frac{1}{3}X - \frac{1}{8}\left(\frac{1}{xy}\right) + x^2 \sqrt{x^3}$$

$$\pi = 3.14$$

$$x = 2\sin y_a$$

$$z = \frac{1}{\sqrt{2}\pi}$$

$$\frac{d\frac{1}{3}}{dx}$$

$$ax + bx + cx = 0$$

14:00

Highest pain threshold

15:00 - 18:00

Best time to exercise

21:30 - 23:00

Easiest time to fall asleep

Your suprachiasmatic nucleus ensures your body temperature and hormone levels follow a regular timetable, even if you don't know the time yourself.

Biggest muscle
gluteus maximus

A pair of *gluteus maximus* muscles move your thighs and hips, and help you stand after sitting down.

Widest muscle
latissimus dorsi

A pair of fan-like muscles that stretch from the lower back to each shoulder.

These muscles allow your arms and shoulders to move in many positions.

Muscle that exerts greatest pressure
masseter

The jaw muscles on either side of your face clamp your teeth together for chewing and cutting food.

Longest muscle
sartorius

A pair of thin strap-like muscles that run from each hip to below each knee.

The name *sartorius* comes from the Latin word for tailor, because it was common for tailors to sew cross-legged.

Muscle with strongest pulling force
soleus

This pair of calf muscles pulls to keep your body upright. You also use them for standing on tip-toe or pointing your toes.

Length: up to 24 inches in adults

You use your *sartorius* muscles for bending, rotating, straightening and crossing your legs.

22 More than half your body...

is made up of oxygen.

There are 94 chemical elements that make up everything in nature. But most of your body is made of just **six** of them.

Chemical make-up of your body

- **65%** Oxygen
- **18%** Carbon
- **10%** Hydrogen
- **3%** Nitrogen
- **1%** Calcium
- **1%** Phosphorus
- **2%** Other elements

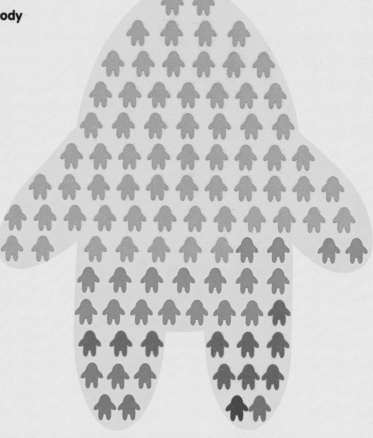

A human cell

Most of your body is made up of **cells**. Cells are made up of a mix of working parts that sit in a fluid called **cytoplasm**.

Cytoplasm

Nucleus

Four elements make up most of each cell.

The cytoplasm is mostly **oxygen** and **hydrogen** (combined as water).

Carbon is in all parts inside the cell.

The biggest part of most cells is called the **nucleus**. It contains a chemical called DNA, which holds **nitrogen**.

23 Your body contains...
poisons and precious metals.

Just 2% of your body is made up of small amounts of over 50 different elements, some of which you probably wouldn't expect to find beneath your own skin.

Titanium is a very strong metal. It's used to make planes.

Uranium is a dangerous radioactive metal. Many nuclear bombs contain it.

Arsenic and **mercury** are poisonous. They are deadly in larger quantities.

Lead is used in bullets.

Silver and **gold**

HUMAN BODY MIXTURE: OTHER ELEMENTS

barium
rubidium
selenium
manganese
nickel
lanthanum
copper
zinc
cerium
vanadium
tantalum
aluminum
germanium
cadmium
cobalt
tungsten
gallium
indium
yttrium
antimony
tin
molybdenum
potassium
beryllium
niobium
sulfur
sodium
strontium
silver
boron
lead
lithium
uranium
fluorine
silicon
gold
samarium
chlorine
titanium
mercury
scandium
tellurium
zirconium
iodine
chromium
thallium
magnesium
arsenic
cesium
bismuth
thorium

There's enough **iron** in your body to make a nail the same size as your little finger.

24 Your eyes are full of tears...

even when you're not crying.

Your eyes need to stay moist all the time, so they produce a steady stream of tears. Crying is what happens when you produce more tears than normal.

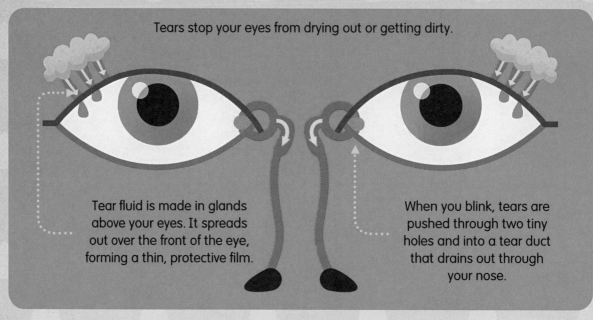

Tears stop your eyes from drying out or getting dirty.

Tear fluid is made in glands above your eyes. It spreads out over the front of the eye, forming a thin, protective film.

When you blink, tears are pushed through two tiny holes and into a tear duct that drains out through your nose.

When you *cry*, you produce extra tears. Your tear ducts overflow, causing tears to spill down your cheeks. There are two types of crying tears:

Reflex tears

When something foreign gets into your eye, you produce lots of **reflex tears**.

Onions contain a chemical which irritates your eyes. Reflex tears wash away that chemical, soothing your eyes.

Emotional tears

The tears you cry because of pain, sadness or joy are called **emotional tears**. They contain hormones and even painkillers not found in reflex tears.

No one knows how it works, but these tears do help to cheer people up.

25 Your heart could fill...

an oil supertanker with blood.

Over a lifetime of 80 years, your heart would pump about 54 million gallons of blood around your body.

In **one heartbeat** (just under a second), your heart pumps about **2.5oz** of blood – around **a third of a cup**.

In **one minute**, your heart beats about **70 times** and pumps enough blood to fill

23
cups

In **one day**, your heart pumps enough blood to fill about

39
bathtubs

In **one year**, your heart pumps enough blood to fill about

1
Olympic swimming pool

Over **80 years**, your heart pumps enough blood to fill

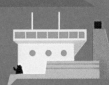

1
oil supertanker

26 The four vital signs...

tell doctors how healthy you are.

Four measurements known as **vital signs** help doctors make a quick diagnosis of your general health. The vital signs are **pulse rate**, **breathing rate**, **body temperature** and **blood pressure**.

Healthy vital signs for an average adult at rest

Pulse rate

60-100 beats per minute

Breathing rate

16-20 breaths per minute

Body temperature

97.7-99.5°F

Blood pressure

approx. 120/80 mmHg (see opposite)

In hospitals special machines can be used to monitor a patient's vital signs.

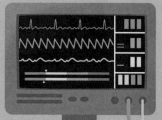

Nurses record these vital signs on a chart, to give doctors a quick update on each patient's recovery.

Your pulse and breathing rates are closely related. If they're too high, the flow of oxygen around your body could be restricted, causing the following symptoms:

Chest pains

Dizziness

Shortness of breath

If your **pulse rate** is too high, your heart might not have time to fill with blood between each beat, reducing blood flow around your body.

If your **breathing rate** is too high, it could mean there's a problem with your lungs or heart such as pneumonia or heart failure.

If your **body temperature** rises or falls by just 1 degree, it can have serious consequences for your health.

Blood pressure is measured in millimeters of mercury (mmHg). This is because the original blood pressure gauges contained mercury.

Medical emergency

106
Fainting 104
Dehydration 102   TOO HIGH
Sweating 100

(°F)   HEALTHY

96 Shivering
95 Numbness

TOO LOW

93 Blueness
91 Confusion
89

Medical emergency

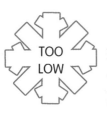

Blood pressure comes as two readings:

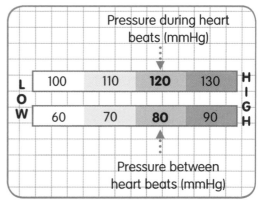

	Pressure during heart beats (mmHg)			
L O W	100	110	**120**	130
L O W	60	70	**80**	90

H I G H

Pressure between heart beats (mmHg)

High blood pressure has no obvious symptoms, but it can lead to serious conditions such as heart disease if it's not treated.

27 The language you speak...

affects the way you sneeze.

Sneezes and coughs are examples of **vegetative sounds**, some of the first noises newborn babies make. You can't stop yourself from making them, but you can learn to control them a little, so they often sound different from person to person. They can even be affected by the language you speak.

The sound people make as they sneeze is especially variable, because it's such a complicated process.

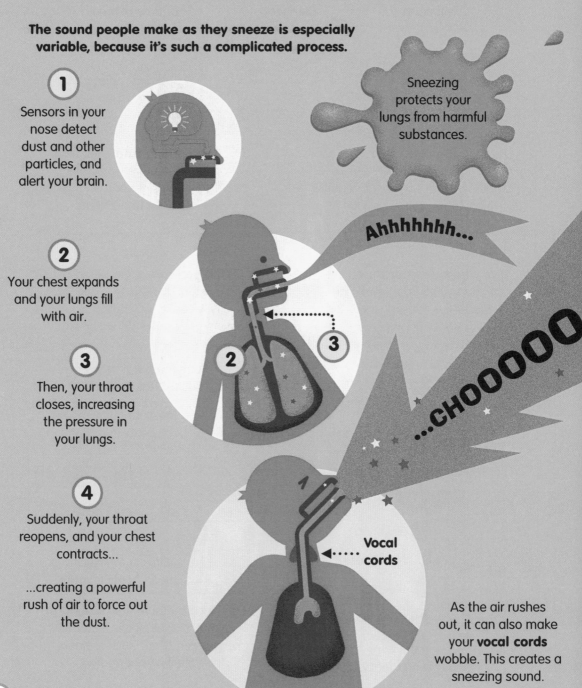

1 Sensors in your nose detect dust and other particles, and alert your brain.

Sneezing protects your lungs from harmful substances.

Ahhhhhhh...

2 Your chest expands and your lungs fill with air.

3 Then, your throat closes, increasing the pressure in your lungs.

...CHOOOOOO

4 Suddenly, your throat reopens, and your chest contracts...

...creating a powerful rush of air to force out the dust.

Vocal cords

As the air rushes out, it can also make your **vocal cords** wobble. This creates a sneezing sound.

As a sneeze passes through your vocal cords, you can alter the way it sounds.

1

You can make the sound louder or softer.

2

You can vocalize the sound.

Without thinking, many people make their sneezes sound the way a typical sneeze is described in their native laguage.

OOOO!

Ecci!
(Italian)

Achoo!
(English)

Ha-ching!
(Filipino)

Hakushon!
(Japanese)

Apchkhee!
(Russian)

28 Pins and needles...

can cure headaches and bad backs.

Some ancient forms of medicine are still used today. One example, called **acupuncture**, involves sticking needles into specific parts of your body. It can be used to treat lots of conditions, but it's most effective at treating pain.

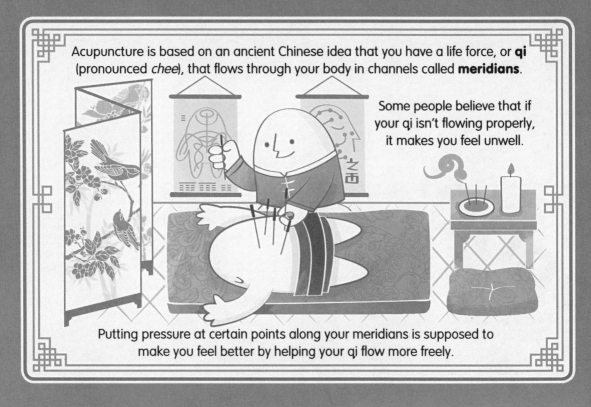

Acupuncture is based on an ancient Chinese idea that you have a life force, or **qi** (pronounced *chee*), that flows through your body in channels called **meridians**.

Some people believe that if your qi isn't flowing properly, it makes you feel unwell.

Putting pressure at certain points along your meridians is supposed to make you feel better by helping your qi flow more freely.

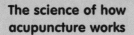

The science of how acupuncture works

Pressure from the needles stimulates nerves under the skin...

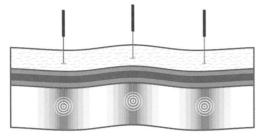

...causing the body to produce pain relieving hormones known as **endorphins**.

When it's performed by trained experts, acupuncture can help the following symptoms:

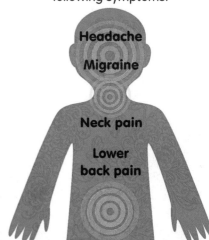

Headache

Migraine

Neck pain

Lower back pain

29 The oldest tattoos in the world...
were probably prehistoric pain relief.

In 1991, an ancient mummy was discovered in the Alps after being preserved in ice for over 5,000 years. The mummy, nicknamed Ötzi, was covered in the world's earliest known tattoos. Scientists believe they served a medical purpose.

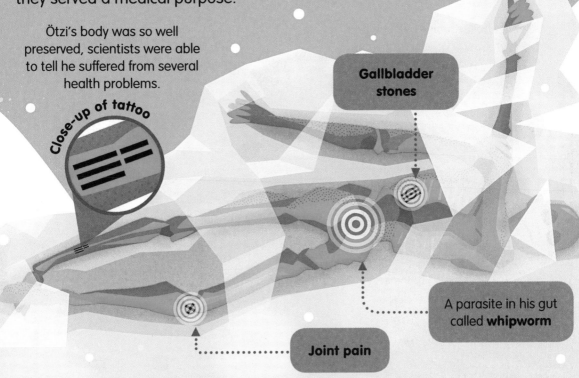

Ötzi's body was so well preserved, scientists were able to tell he suffered from several health problems.

Close-up of tattoo

Gallbladder stones

A parasite in his gut called **whipworm**

Joint pain

Tattoos are made by inserting needles under the skin. Each needle prick is filled with dyes, that leave a permanent mark.

Ötzi's body was covered in **61 tattoos**.

They were placed in areas where his ailments would have caused him pain, or around pressure points often used in acupuncture.

Scientists think it's likely Ötzi's tattoos were created at least partly to help him manage his pain.

30 Just because you can see it...

doesn't mean it's really there.

Human brains are capable of a phenomenon called **hallucinating**, during which they see, hear, feel or smell things that aren't actually there. Hallucinatons often seem completely real, even though they aren't.

Most hallucinations start when something goes wrong in a person's brain.

Problems in a part called the **fusiform gyrus** can make your brain 'see' strange-looking faces – even when there are no people around.

Some **drugs** can have dangerous effects on the balance of chemicals in the brain, causing strange hallucinations.

Holes or tumors in the **occipital lobe** can make a person think they are interacting with people who aren't there.

Some types of a brain disease called **epilepsy** can make people 'smell' or 'taste' things that aren't really there.

Between 10% and 40% of people experience hallucinations in their lifetime.

A brain disease called **schizophrenia** often makes people 'hear' imaginary voices talking to them.

31 Your teeth are harder...

than steel.

You can measure exactly how hard different substances are using something called the **Mohs scale of hardness**. The hardest thing that your body produces is **enamel**, a white substance that covers the outside of your teeth.

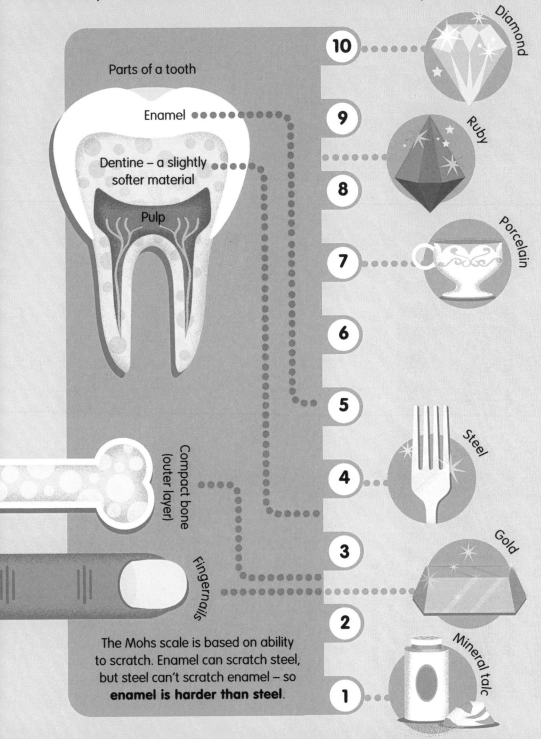

Parts of a tooth

Enamel

Dentine – a slightly softer material

Pulp

Compact bone (outer layer)

Fingernails

10 · · · · · · · Diamond

9

8 · · · · · · · Ruby

7 · · · · · · · Porcelain

6

5

4 · · · · · · · Steel

3

2 · · · · · · · Gold

1 · · · · · · · Mineral talc

The Mohs scale is based on ability to scratch. Enamel can scratch steel, but steel can't scratch enamel – so **enamel is harder than steel**.

32 You probably can't...

wiggle your ears.

There are some things that almost everyone can do with their bodies, some that only a few people can do, and some that no matter how hard you try, are practically impossible. Which of these can *you do?*

Even if you can't snap your fingers, you could probably teach yourself.

Most people can **whistle, cross their eyes,** and **snap their fingers.**

Rolling your tongue is different. If you can't do it naturally, it's very difficult to learn.

Raising one **eyebrow** is hard to master.

Only 1 in 10 people can **wiggle their ears.**

You can't **hum with your nose plugged,** because air has to come out of your nose.

Your brain finds it difficult to do these two things at once.

Try writing the number 6 while moving your foot clockwise.

You can't **sneeze with your eyes open.** The muscles controlling your eyelids tense automatically.

Aaaachooo!

33 Blushing is only human...

and only humans blush.

Blushing means turning red in the face as a result of stressful feelings such as shame or embarrassment. All humans blush, and we're the only creatures who do it.

Scientists don't know exactly why humans respond this way, but they do know how the process works.

(1)
In stressful situations your body produces a hormone called **adrenaline**.

(2)
Adrenaline increases the oxygen circulating in your body. You breathe more quickly...

...your heart beats faster...

...and your blood vessels grow wider.

(3)
As your blood vessels widen, more blood flows through them.

This makes them appear redder on the outside and feel hotter on the inside.

Close-up of a blushing cheek

The blood vessels in your cheeks are especially responsive to **adrenaline**. They're packed in tightly, just under the skin, so blushing shows more in your cheeks than anywhere else.

your brain is.

To stay alive, your body needs to remember to do all sorts of things, from breathing to digesting food. Luckily, you don't have to worry about any of this an unconscious part of your nervous system does it for you.
This is known as your **autonomic nervous system** (ANS).

Different parts of your ANS take control depending on what your body needs.

• One part of your ANS is active during normal situations.

• Another part takes over in emergencies, when you need to be alert.

Your ANS is controlled by a gland in your brain called the **hypothalamus**...

...your **brain stem**...

...and the nerves that run down your back: your **spinal cord**.

Pupils narrow

Pupils open wide

Heart beats normally

Heart beats very fast

Core body temperature kept at the same level

Adrenaline released to react to things more quickly

Digestion active

Digestion put on hold

Some people *can* learn to control many of these abilities. But your brain stem and spine will always take over in emergencies.

Deep, slow breathing

Fast breathing

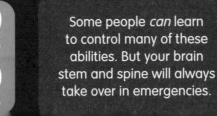

35 Your body can attack...

healthy cells as well as germs.

Your body fights harmful germs, such as bacteria or viruses, using its **immune system**. However, in some cases, your immune system may start to destroy healthy cells by mistake. This is called an **autoimmune disorder**.

How your immune system works:

1 Germs carry tiny parts called **antigens**. When they enter your body...

2 ...your immune system immediately produces **antibodies**.

3 Antibodies can attack antigens...

4 ...and kill the germs that carry them, making you well again.

If you have an autoimmune disorder...

...your immune system can't tell the difference between *healthy* cells and *harmful* antigens.

There are more than 80 types of autoimmune disorders, including **multiple sclerosis** and **celiac disease**.

Antigen

Healthy cell

As a result, your body produces antibodies that destroy healthy cells instead.

36 Your eyes might turn yellow...

if your liver isn't working properly.

Your liver helps break down a yellowish waste substance in your blood called **bilirubin**. But if your liver is not working properly, bilirubin stays in your blood and makes your skin and the whites of your eyes turn yellow.

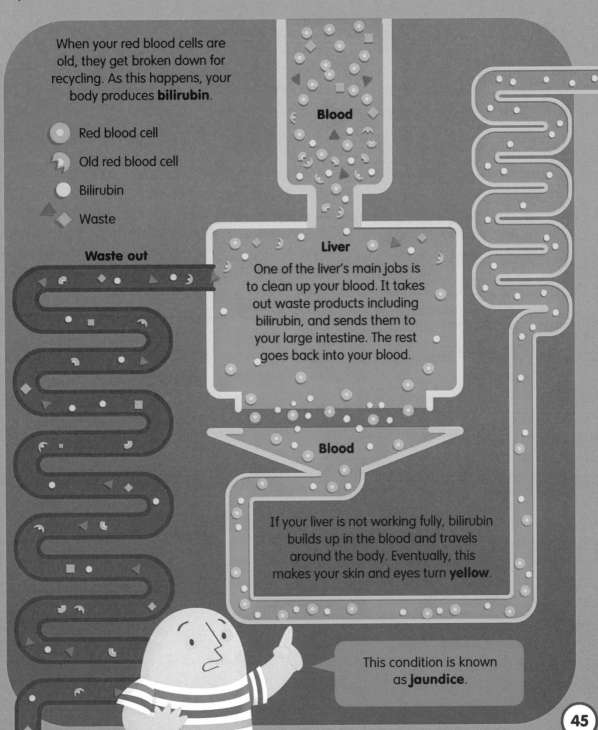

When your red blood cells are old, they get broken down for recycling. As this happens, your body produces **bilirubin**.

- Red blood cell
- Old red blood cell
- Bilirubin
- Waste

Blood

Waste out

Liver

One of the liver's main jobs is to clean up your blood. It takes out waste products including bilirubin, and sends them to your large intestine. The rest goes back into your blood.

Blood

If your liver is not working fully, bilirubin builds up in the blood and travels around the body. Eventually, this makes your skin and eyes turn **yellow**.

This condition is known as **jaundice**.

37 Too much sugar...

might make you lose your feet.

People with a disease called **diabetes** have too much **glucose** – a type of sugar – in their blood. This can affect the health of their entire body, especially their feet.

Normally, your pancreas produces an enzyme called **insulin**.

This allows your body's cells to absorb glucose from your blood.

But two types of diabetes can disrupt this process:

Type 1
The pancreas makes very little **insulin**.

Type 2
The body still makes insulin, but is unable to use it to process glucose.

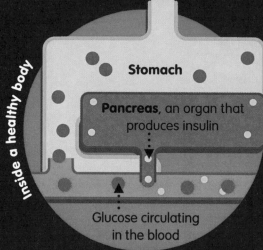

Inside a healthy body

Stomach

Pancreas, an organ that produces insulin

Glucose circulating in the blood

Living with diabetes

1 Everyone gets glucose from food and drink, especially things that contain lots of sugar.

2 Over time, the high level of glucose in the blood damages the blood vessels.

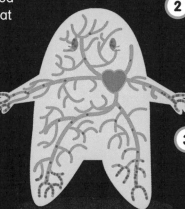

3 This especially affects the edges of the circulatory system, such as the **eyeballs** and **feet**.

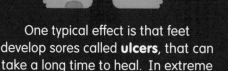

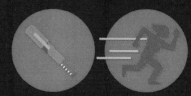

4 One typical effect is that feet develop sores called **ulcers**, that can take a long time to heal. In extreme cases, a foot may need to be cut off.

5 Fortunately, people with diabetes can control the disease with insulin injections, medicine, exercising and eating a healthy, balanced diet.

38 Human DNA...

can turn moss into medicine.

Manufacturing insulin is complex and expensive, but is vital for some people with diabetes. A new method has been discovered that may one day make insulin readily available. It works by combining human DNA with moss DNA...

Human DNA **Moss DNA** **Altered moss DNA**

(1) Extract DNA from one kind of moss – *Physcomitrella patens*.

(2) Insert the section of human DNA that creates insulin into the moss DNA.

(3) Insert the altered moss DNA into the original moss.

(4) The moss grows and reproduces. As it does, it creates **insulin**.

All moss needs to grow is water, light and plant food.

Chemists could extract insulin from the moss, and turn it into medicine for diabetics.

This method is likely to **cost far less** and **produce far more** than current methods.

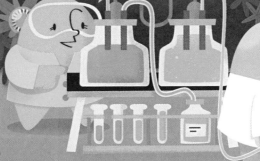

39 Blood can spurt...
up to 30 feet through the air.

How far and fast blood flows from a wound depends on the size of the cut blood vessel and the pressure of blood within it. Bloods flows slowest through **capillaries** – small blood vessels – and fastest through **arteries.**

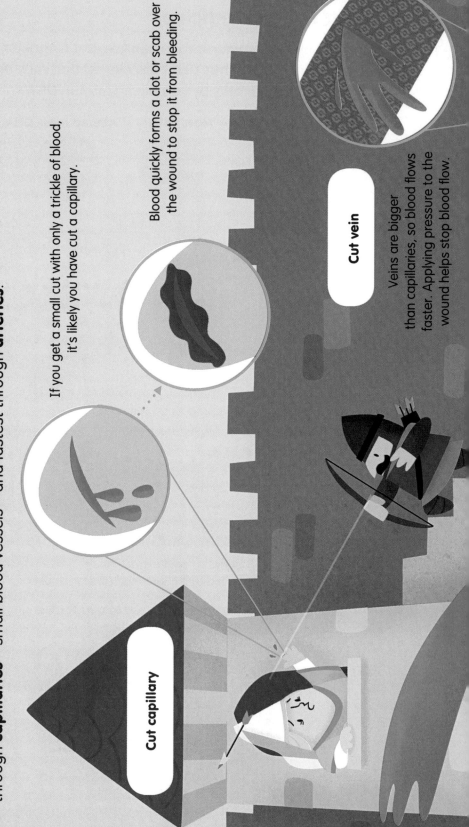

If you get a small cut with only a trickle of blood, it's likely you have cut a capillary.

Blood quickly forms a clot or scab over the wound to stop it from bleeding.

Cut capillary

Cut vein

Veins are bigger than capillaries, so blood flows faster. Applying pressure to the wound helps stop blood flow.

Blood oozes steadily from veins.

Applying firm pressure to the wound for about 15 minutes may help stop blood flow.

Cut artery

Blood spurts from cut arteries in bursts, with each beat of the heart.

Arteries take blood directly from the heart to other parts of the body. They also have elastic walls to keep up the high pressure of the blood pumping through them. This is what makes you lose blood so rapidly from a cut artery.

40 Optical illusions...

are tricking your *brain*, not your eyes.

Optical illusions are images designed to trick your brain into seeing something that isn't really there. Because of the way your brain works, even when you know the trick, it's almost impossible to train your eyes *not* to see the illusion.

Look at these two circles.

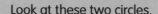

The left circle is sticking out and the right circle is pushing in. Or is it the other way round?

It depends how you look at them. Different people see different things.

The truth is that neither of them is really sticking in or out. They're just flat, two-dimensional (2-D), pictures.

They're bumps!

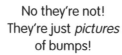

No they're not! They're just *pictures* of bumps!

From years of experience of seeing the real, **three-dimensional world**, your brain automatically sees the darker patches as shadows. It's almost impossible to make your brain see these illusions as 2-D drawings.

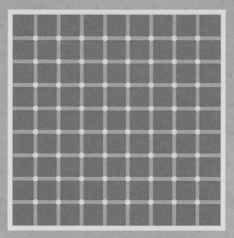

Can you see dark dots appearing
on top of the yellow circles?

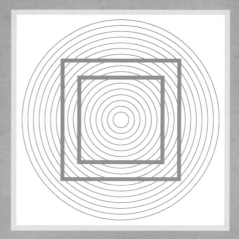

Do the two red squares have
straight sides or curved sides?

All these 2-D
pictures are
playing tricks on
your mind.

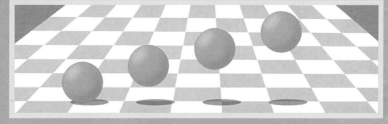

Are these balls up in the air..?

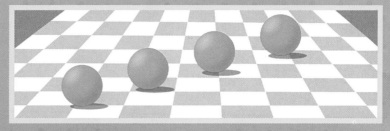

...while these are down on the ground?

Look at the gray lines. Are they parallel or not?

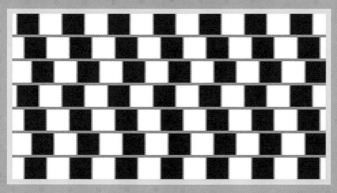

Trying to force your
brain to cope with two
conflicting ideas at the
same time is hard work.

Find a ruler with a flat edge and you can check that these
lines really *are* parallel, even though they appear slanted.

41 Surgeons use shockwaves...

to break up gut-blocking bezoars.

Bezoars are hard, solid lumps that can form inside your gut. They're made when fibers from undigested material such as hair or food become tangled up. These hard chunks can block your digestive tract.

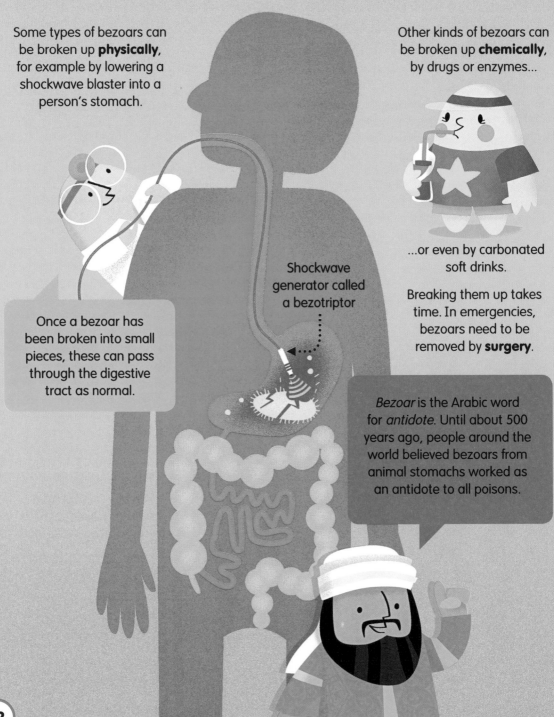

Some types of bezoars can be broken up **physically**, for example by lowering a shockwave blaster into a person's stomach.

Other kinds of bezoars can be broken up **chemically**, by drugs or enzymes...

...or even by carbonated soft drinks.

Breaking them up takes time. In emergencies, bezoars need to be removed by **surgery**.

Shockwave generator called a bezotriptor

Once a bezoar has been broken into small pieces, these can pass through the digestive tract as normal.

Bezoar is the Arabic word for *antidote*. Until about 500 years ago, people around the world believed bezoars from animal stomachs worked as an antidote to all poisons.

42 Tricking your mind...

can cure your body.

Sometimes, patients who are given false medicines, known as **placebos**, show a real improvement in their condition. This is known as the **placebo effect**. Doctors think it works because patients who *expect* to get better are more likely to spur their brains to try to fix a problem internally.

Placebos come in many different forms:

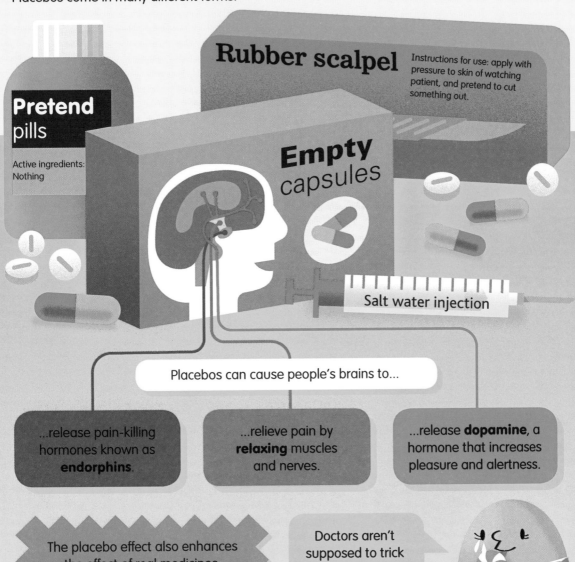

Pretend pills

Active ingredients: Nothing

Rubber scalpel

Instructions for use: apply with pressure to skin of watching patient, and pretend to cut something out.

Empty capsules

Salt water injection

Placebos can cause people's brains to...

| ...release pain-killing hormones known as **endorphins**. | ...relieve pain by **relaxing** muscles and nerves. | ...release **dopamine**, a hormone that increases pleasure and alertness. |

The placebo effect also enhances the effect of real medicines.

Doctors have found that patients feel less benefit from real painkillers if they don't know they've taken them.

Doctors aren't supposed to trick their patients. Instead they use placebos to help check how well real medicines work.

53

43 Bleeding, sweating and vomiting...

were once standard medical treatments.

Around 500 years ago, doctors across Europe followed an ancient Greek theory for diagnosing and treating diseases. It was based on the belief that the human body contains four basic fluids, or **humors**. If a person was unwell, it was because these humors were out of balance.

The four humors

Blood	Yellow bile	Black bile	Phlegm
Associated with: **heart or liver pain**	Associated with: **anger, aggression**	Associated with: **tumors, pain**	Associated with: **depression, poor breathing**

Treatment

There were only two basic forms of treatment for any problem:

Purging

Making people bleed, sweat or vomit, to remove excess humor.

Changing diet

Prescribing specific food and drink, especially herbs, that were thought to replenish a 'missing' humor.

Some ancient herbal remedies have been scientifically proven to work. But purging is almost always very bad for people.

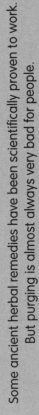

44 Talking and chewing...

can keep your ears clean.

Your ears clean themselves all the time to protect you from infection. This process is called **epithelial migration**. It's very slow, but you can speed it up by moving your jaw, for example when you talk or eat.

Epithelial migration takes place in the **ear canal**, a tube that connects your eardrum to your outer ear.

Ear canal

Eardrum

Epithelial migration works like a very slow conveyor belt, with blocks of new skin cells pushing old ones outwards.

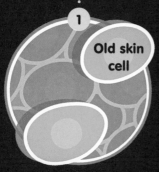

1

Old skin cell

New skin cells form in the eardrum. They push old skin cells out along the ear canal.

2

Glands along the canal produce a sticky material called **earwax**.

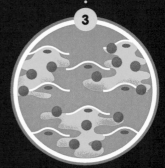

3

Earwax traps dirt and contains chemicals that kill bacteria.

Earwax coats tiny
hairs all along
the canal.

4

The hairs become
sticky, trapping dirt
more easily.

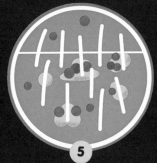

5

Old skin cells push
dirty earwax towards
the outer ear.

6

The skin cells move at roughly the speed that fingernails grow.
In an average adult that's 0.3mm (0.1 inches) a month.

Outer
ear

So eating this
sandwich could help
my ears keep clean?

Yes! Your jaw joint is right next
to the ear canal, so epithelial
migration speeds up whenever
you move your jaw.

Eardrum

Ear canal

Outer ear

Jaw joint

45 A hug from a machine...

can be as calming as a real hug.

High school student Temple Grandin built herself a **hug machine** – a mechanical device that could squeeze her whole body, similar to getting a hug from a person. She proved that such a machine could help calm people who are feeling anxious.

Her autism meant she was easily upset by loud noises and by being touched.

1947
Grandin was born to a wealthy family in Boston, Massachusetts, USA.

1949
At age two, she was not yet talking. She began to show signs of a condition known as **autism**.

1961
Grandin was sent to her aunt's ranch in Arizona. She was fascinated to watch farmers calming their cattle using squeezing machines.

1960s
Grandin built her own squeezing machine to help control her anxiety. She found it worked on other people and animals, too.

Today, hug machines can play a part in therapy for autism, and a condition known as ADHD.

46 Tiny arachnids...

live inside your face.

All sorts of tiny creatures live in or on the human body. Creatures called **face mites** live in tiny holes in your skin, called **pores**, mostly around your eyes and nose. Face mites are *arachnids* – eight-legged creepy crawlies.

The are two types of mites that live on people's faces.

Demodex brevis

Demodex folliculorum

Face mites eat a grease called **sebum** that the skin produces. Most people never notice them.

Demodex brevis live around the tiny hairs that grow from your face, especially your eyelashes.

Demodex folliculorum live in the glands around follicles, where sebum is made.

Follicle – a hole hair grows from.

47 Babies don't have...

wrist bones.

Bones develop from a softer substance called **cartilage**. A baby's skeleton isn't fully developed when it's born, and some parts, such as the wrists, are still cartilage.

Over time, most of the cartilage hardens into bone. This process is called **ossification**. It continues until the age of around 25.

Unlike bone, cartilage doesn't show up on an X-ray. It looks as if there's nothing there.

X-ray of a baby's wrist

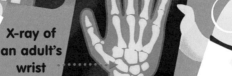

X-ray of an adult's wrist

48 Millions of people take...

a mind-altering drug every day.

Coffee, tea and many cola and energy drinks all contain **caffeine** – a drug that has a rapid effect on your brain.

If you drink a cup of coffee, caffeine passes into your stomach then quickly enters your blood.

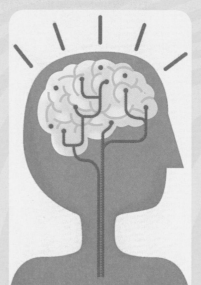

Blood flows to your brain. Caffeine reacts with chemicals in your brain to stop you from feeling sleepy.

Messages between your brain and your body speed up, making you feel more alert.

If you're used to a daily dose of 100mg of caffeine – the amount in one big cup of coffee – you can feel unwell if you stop having it.

The ill effects, known as **withdrawal symptoms**, include:

Bad mood
Headache
Lack of concentration

Many people have **caffeine** without realizing it.
You can find it in lots of products:

| Tea | Coffee | Colas | Painkillers | Energy drinks | Chocolate |

Cancer isn't *a* disease...

it's more than 200 different diseases.

Almost any part of the body can be affected by various forms of something called **cancer**, a group of diseases that begins inside cells. The name 'cancer' was given by a Greek physician named Hippocrates over 2,300 years ago.

Hippocrates wrote that the veins he found inside tumors looked like pincers. He used a Greek word, *karkinos*.

Cancer means crab in Latin.

Around the world, more than
12.5 million
people are diagnosed with cancer every year.

But there are at least
28 million
people alive today who have survived their cancer.

How cancer works

Healthy cells

Tumor

Cancerous cells

Cancer may begin in almost any type of cell. Doctors can often treat it, especially if it's discovered early on.

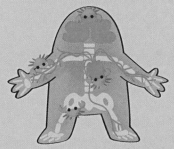

Cells are supposed to multiply. Cancer happens when a few cells multiply out of control.

Cancerous cells can form lumps called **tumors**, and may spread to other parts of the body.

Carcinomas – cancers affecting organs and glands

Sarcomas – cancers of tissues such as bone and muscle

Lymphoma – cancer of the immune system

Leukemia – cancer of the blood

50 People are gassier...

on planes.

The average person passes gas 10 times a day. But on a plane, changes in air pressure make this happen even more often.

Why do you pass gas?

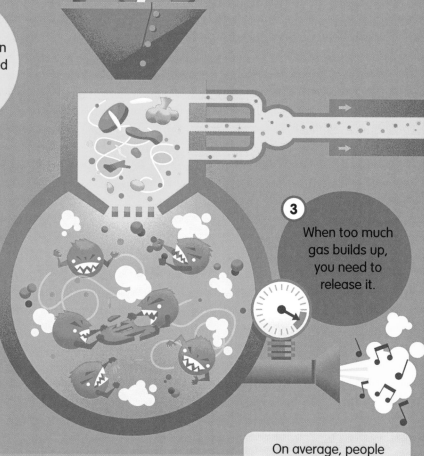

1 When you eat, most food is broken down and absorbed by the intestines.

2 But parts of food that the intestines can't digest are broken down by bacteria. This produces lots of gases – some of them smelly.

3 When too much gas builds up, you need to release it.

High-flying gas

As the plane goes higher, the air pressure in the cabin gets lower.

This makes any air inside your body expand, until it has to be released.

Pardon me!

On average, people on planes pass gas nearly three times more than usual.

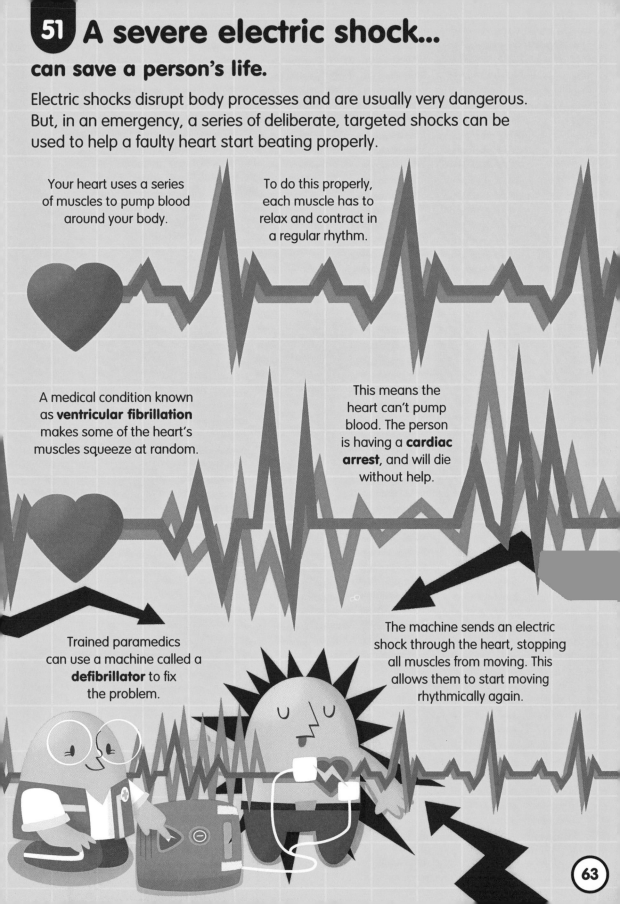

51 A severe electric shock...

can save a person's life.

Electric shocks disrupt body processes and are usually very dangerous. But, in an emergency, a series of deliberate, targeted shocks can be used to help a faulty heart start beating properly.

Your heart uses a series of muscles to pump blood around your body.

To do this properly, each muscle has to relax and contract in a regular rhythm.

A medical condition known as **ventricular fibrillation** makes some of the heart's muscles squeeze at random.

This means the heart can't pump blood. The person is having a **cardiac arrest**, and will die without help.

Trained paramedics can use a machine called a **defibrillator** to fix the problem.

The machine sends an electric shock through the heart, stopping all muscles from moving. This allows them to start moving rhythmically again.

52 The world's first nose job...

was performed at least 5,000 years ago.

Medical texts discovered in archeological sites from Ancient Egypt reveal that surgeons performed all sorts of operations, including **rhinoplasty** – deliberate reshaping of a person's nose.

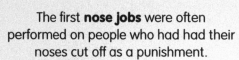

The first **nose jobs** were often performed on people who had had their noses cut off as a punishment.

Ancient Egyptians may have invented the first **dental braces**, too.

They threaded gold wire through holes drilled into teeth. Tightening the thread would, over time, close up gaps between teeth.

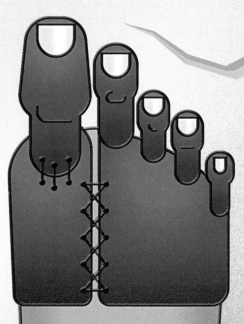

The world's oldest surviving **prosthesis** also belongs to Ancient Egypt: a set of wooden toes.

53 The way you eat your food...

changes the shape of your face.

Most people around the world today have a slight **overbite** – their top teeth hang slightly in front of their bottom teeth. Some experts think this is probably the result of cutting food up before eating it.

Old way of eating: tearing chunks of food off using front teeth

New way of eating: cutting up food first, then chewing small pieces

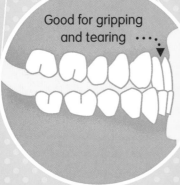

Good for gripping and tearing ····▼

Good for chewing small mouthfuls·· ·

Skulls from people who lived before the invention of forks and chopsticks consistently show teeth that line up.

Skulls dating from more recent times consistently show teeth forming an overbite.

Experts suggest that people unconsciously push their teeth into an overbite to help them chew small pieces of food. Over time, this changes the shape of their jaws.

54 Blondes have more...

hairs on their heads.

Each of the hairs on your body grows through a narrow passage called a **follicle**. People with blonde hair usually have more follicles (and hairs) on their scalp than people with hair of other colors.

The shape of the follicle decides whether the hair will be curly or straight.

A tightly curved follicle causes the hair to be **very curly or coiled**.

If the follicle is slightly curved, the hair will be **wavy**.

A straight follicle produces **straight** hair.

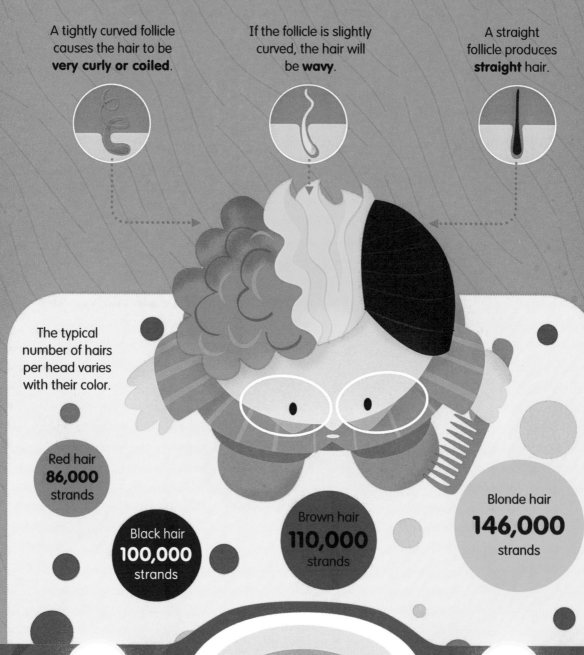

The typical number of hairs per head varies with their color.

Red hair
86,000
strands

Black hair
100,000
strands

Brown hair
110,000
strands

Blonde hair
146,000
strands

Running and jumping...
your blood pumping.

amount of blood your heart pumps each minute is known as your **iac output** (CO). Not only does exercise increase your CO dramatically, o changes the way it's distributed around your body.

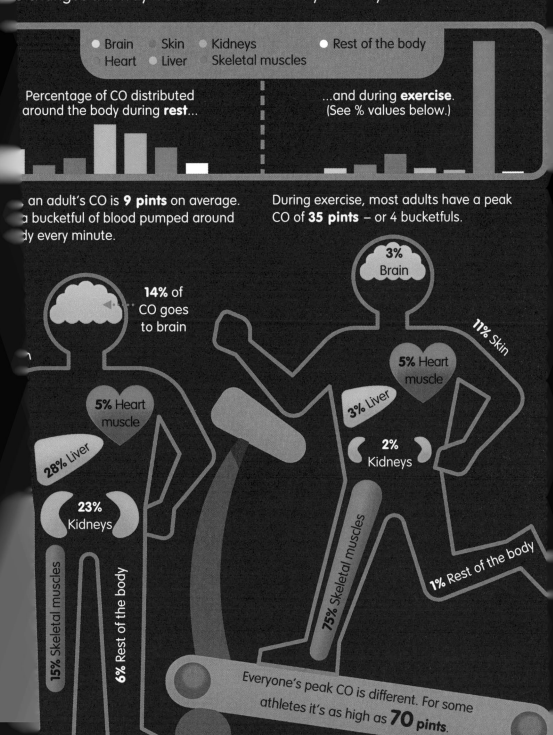

- Brain
- Heart
- Skin
- Liver
- Kidneys
- Skeletal muscles
- Rest of the body

Percentage of CO distributed around the body during **rest**...

...and during **exercise**. (See % values below.)

an adult's CO is **9 pints** on average. a bucketful of blood pumped around dy every minute.

During exercise, most adults have a peak CO of **35 pints** – or 4 bucketfuls.

3% Brain

14% of CO goes to brain

5% Heart muscle

11% Skin

5% Heart muscle

3% Liver

28% Liver

2% Kidneys

23% Kidneys

15% Skeletal muscles

6% Rest of the body

75% Skeletal muscles

1% Rest of the body

Everyone's peak CO is different. For some athletes it's as high as **70** pints.

56 Human beings...

are the only animals with chins.

Your chin is part of a bone on your lower jaw, called the **mandible**. Many animals have mandibles, but only humans have a bump at the end that sticks out. Humans are unique in a handful of other ways, too...

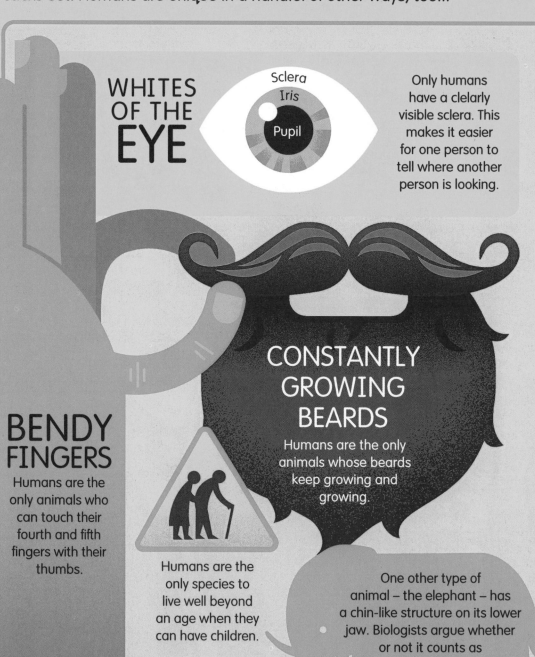

WHITES OF THE EYE

Sclera
Iris
Pupil

Only humans have a clelarly visible sclera. This makes it easier for one person to tell where another person is looking.

CONSTANTLY GROWING BEARDS

Humans are the only animals whose beards keep growing and growing.

BENDY FINGERS

Humans are the only animals who can touch their fourth and fifth fingers with their thumbs.

Humans are the only species to live well beyond an age when they can have children.

One other type of animal – the elephant – has a chin-like structure on its lower jaw. Biologists argue whether or not it counts as a true chin.

57 Your chin...

is an accident of nature.

No one really knows why humans developed chins. Unlike your jaw, your chin is not necessary for chewing or talking. One popular theory is that chins developed by accident, a by-product of some other bodily development. These by-products are known as **spandrels**.

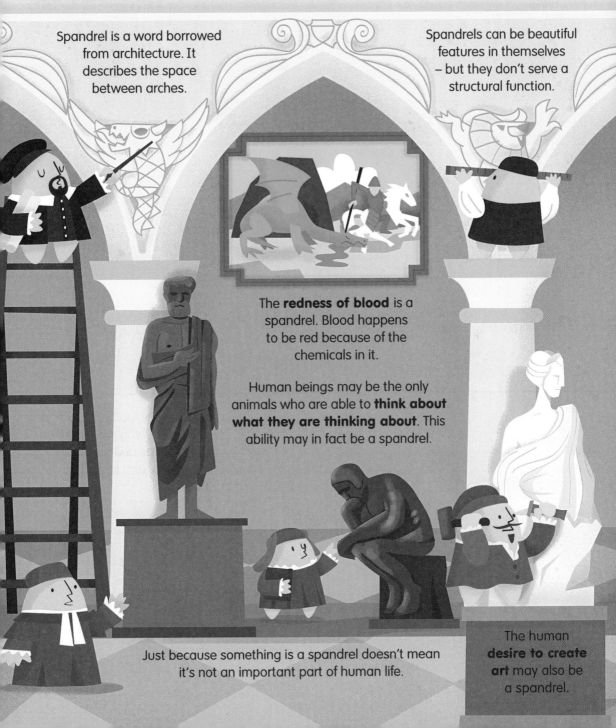

Spandrel is a word borrowed from architecture. It describes the space between arches.

Spandrels can be beautiful features in themselves – but they don't serve a structural function.

The **redness of blood** is a spandrel. Blood happens to be red because of the chemicals in it.

Human beings may be the only animals who are able to **think about what they are thinking about**. This ability may in fact be a spandrel.

Just because something is a spandrel doesn't mean it's not an important part of human life.

The human **desire to create art** may also be a spandrel.

You can't move your fingers...

without moving your arms.

You make parts of your body move using **muscles** which pull on your bones. Most muscles are next to the bones they move, but the muscles that move your fingers are further away, in your forearm. So, whenever you move your fingers, you have to twitch parts of your arms, too.

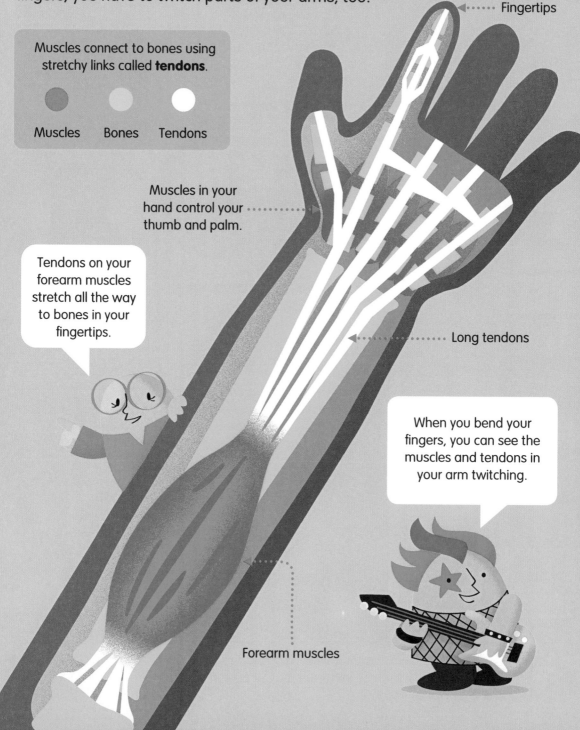

Muscles connect to bones using stretchy links called **tendons**.

Muscles   Bones   Tendons

Fingertips

Muscles in your hand control your thumb and palm.

Tendons on your forearm muscles stretch all the way to bones in your fingertips.

Long tendons

When you bend your fingers, you can see the muscles and tendons in your arm twitching.

Forearm muscles

59 Tummy trouble...
can give you a pain in the shoulder.

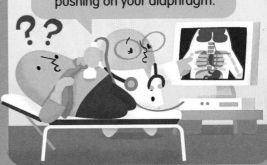

How it happens:
Nerve signals from your diaphragm join with signals from your neck and shoulders before they reach your brain.

Nerve ·········

Diaphragm ·········

Stomach ·········

Sometimes, your brain mixes up the source of the signal, and thinks the pain is coming from elsewhere. This is called **referred pain**.

Referred pain can affect your organs, too:

Some people feel the pain of a heart attack...

...in their shoulder, along their arm and even in their fingertips.

Problems affecting a person's kidneys...

...can cause pain all around their lower back and thighs.

60 Climbing Everest...
can damage your brain.

High up a mountain, the air has less pressure and less oxygen than at sea level. If you climb too high too quickly, your body doesn't have a chance to adapt to the lack of oxygen. This can lead to brain damage.

Mount Everest
29,000 feet

At the top of Mount Everest, air pressure is a third what it is at sea level, and there is only a third the number of oxygen molecules in the air.

As you climb higher, every breath contains fewer oxygen molecules. Climbers need to breathe faster and deeper to get enough oxygen.

Extreme altitude

Climbers may suffer from severe altitude sickness. This can make fluid leak from blood vessels in the lungs and brain, causing damage to brain cells.

Symptoms: vomiting, confusion, memory loss, hallucinations

Above 18,000ft

Given enough time, your body can usually adapt to having less oxygen. This is known as **acclimatization**, and it can take 1-7 days.

Very high altitude

Climbers may suffer from moderate altitude sickness.

Symptoms: headache, nausea shortness of breath, difficulty walking

High altitude

Climbers may suffer from mild altitude sickness.

Symptoms: headache, nausea, dizziness, problems sleeping

Sea level

The sea lies under a large volume of air in the atmosphere.

The feeling of all the air molecules pressing down together is known as **air pressure**.

Above 11,500ft

Above 10,000ft

0ft (Sea level)

61 Your body will sacrifice...

fingers and toes to survive in very cold weather.

To stay alive in freezing temperatures, your body will automatically stop blood flowing to your fingers, toes, ears and other extremities. This may eventually make these parts drop off, but it preserves heat for the rest of your body.

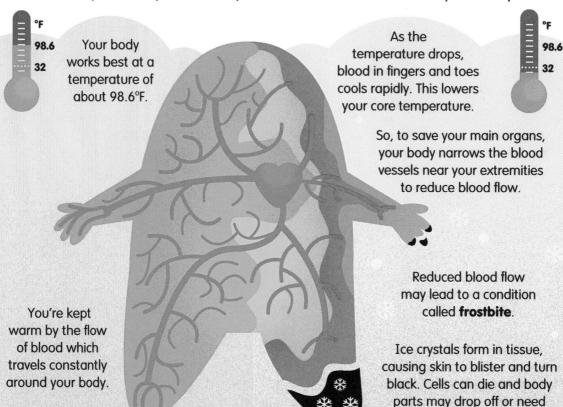

°F
98.6
32

Your body works best at a temperature of about 98.6°F.

As the temperature drops, blood in fingers and toes cools rapidly. This lowers your core temperature.

°F
98.6
32

So, to save your main organs, your body narrows the blood vessels near your extremities to reduce blood flow.

You're kept warm by the flow of blood which travels constantly around your body.

Reduced blood flow may lead to a condition called **frostbite**.

Ice crystals form in tissue, causing skin to blister and turn black. Cells can die and body parts may drop off or need removing to prevent infection.

Many polar explorers and mountaineers have lost body parts due to frostbite.

Beck Weathers
Lost nose, hand, and fingertips climbing Everest, 1996

Sir Ranulph Fiennes
Lost fingertips of left hand in a polar expedition, 2000

Lincoln Hall
Lost one toe and eight fingertips climbing Everest, 2006

Fireflies and humans...

both glow in the dark.

Your body emits light in the same way as animals such as fireflies. But the light humans produce is so weak that you can't see it with the naked eye.

Light from living things is called **bioluminescence**. It's produced when molecules react with each other, making tiny sparks of light called **photons**.

The face produces the most light.

Firefly

The light produced by the human body is a thousand times weaker than light the naked eye can see.

Less light — More light

It can only be detected using an extremely sensitive camera called a CCD (charge-coupled device) in a completely dark room.

These bioluminescent creatures glow so strongly that they can be seen without a CCD.

Glowing squid

Green bomber worm

Crystal jellyfish

Box jellyfish

63 The tallest person ever...

was over five times taller than the shortest.

Human bodies come in all shapes and sizes. Here are some of the most remarkable ever to have existed.

Tallest man
Robert Wadlow,
USA
(1918-1940)
8ft, 11in

Tallest woman
Zeng Jinlian,
China
(1964-1982)
8ft, 1¾in

Average male   5ft, 8in

Average female   5ft, 3in

Shortest man
Chandra Bahadur
Dangi, Nepal
(1939-2015)
1ft, 9.5in

Shortest woman
Pauline Musters,
Netherlands
(1876-1895)
1ft, 11in

Widest tongue
Byron Schlenker, USA
(born 1968)
3.4in

Longest nails (male)
Melvin Boothe, USA
(1948-2009)
32ft, 3in

Longest hair
Xie Qiuping, China
(born 1960)
18ft, 4in

Widest mouth
Francisco Joaquim, Angola (born 1990)
6.69in

Loudest voice
Annalisa Flanagan, UK
(born 1975)
121 decibels

Longest nose
Mehmet Ozyurek, Turkey
(born 1949)
3.46in

Longest tongue
Nick Stoeberl, USA
(born 1990)
3.98in

64 Babies' lungs don't breathe...

until they are born.

In the womb, babies' lungs are full of liquid, so they can't take in oxygen by breathing. Instead, they receive oxygen directly from their mother, through a tube called the **umbilical cord**.

In the womb

The baby is surrounded by a liquid called **amniotic fluid** which also fills its lungs. This fluid protects the baby and helps the lungs to develop.

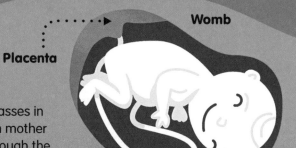

Womb

Placenta

Oxygen passes in blood from mother to baby through the **umbilical cord**.

Amniotic fluid

During birth

Most liquid in the lungs is squeezed out as the baby is being born.

As the baby begins to take in air, any liquid left in its lungs is coughed out or absorbed by the body.

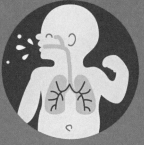

It can take several minutes or even hours for a baby's lungs to start working fully.

After birth

waaaaaaaa

A baby's first cry shows that its lungs have started to work.

65 A hole in the head...
cures madness, they said.

Trepanning, or drilling a hole in the skull, is one of the world's oldest surgical operations. It was once thought that simply having the operation was enough to cure illness, but today it is only used as part of a careful medical procedure.

Ancient operations

Trepanned skulls have been found around the world, some of them dating back more than 8,000 years ago.

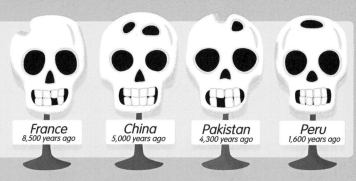

France	China	Pakistan	Peru
8,500 years ago	5,000 years ago	4,300 years ago	1,600 years ago

Medieval madness

Around 600 years ago, trepanning was thought to cure mental illness by releasing demons they believed were trapped inside the head.

You'll be better again in no time.

Trepanning: what to expect

- Patients usually survive
- Provides some pain relief
- Skull heals over time

Disclaimer:
May result in brain damage or death

Trepanning today

There is a modern operation, called a **craniotomy**, that is similar to trepanning.

A piece of skull is cut away in order to operate on the brain.

After the operation, it is put back into place.

Surgeons only perform a craniotomy in serious cases, such as removing a brain tumor.

Listening from the outside...

helps doctors explore your insides.

Doctors use stethoscopes to listen to internal parts of the body, where air or liquids move around. Sometimes they're able to diagnose problems, just by listening out for certain sounds. This is called **auscultation**.

These are some of the **sounds** that doctors listen out for...

THE LUNGS

CREAK!

WHEEZE!

Cause: narrow airways
Possible diagnosis: asthma

Cause: narrowed airways near your voicebox
Possible diagnosis: croup

THE HEART

CRACKLE!

WHOOSH

Cause: blockages in tiny airways popping open
Possible diagnosis: pneumonia

Cause: disturbed (turbulent) blood flow
Possible diagnosis: heart murmur

THE BOWEL

...SILENCE...

Cause: a blockage in the intestines
Possible diagnosis: inflammatory bowel disease (for example, Crohn's disease)

67 Eating ice cream...

can cause *sphenopalatine ganglioneuralgia.*

Eating very cold food can cause a chain reaction that temporarily stimulates pain receptors in your head – commonly called an **ice cream headache** or **brain freeze**. The technical name for this is *sphenopalatine ganglioneuralgia.*

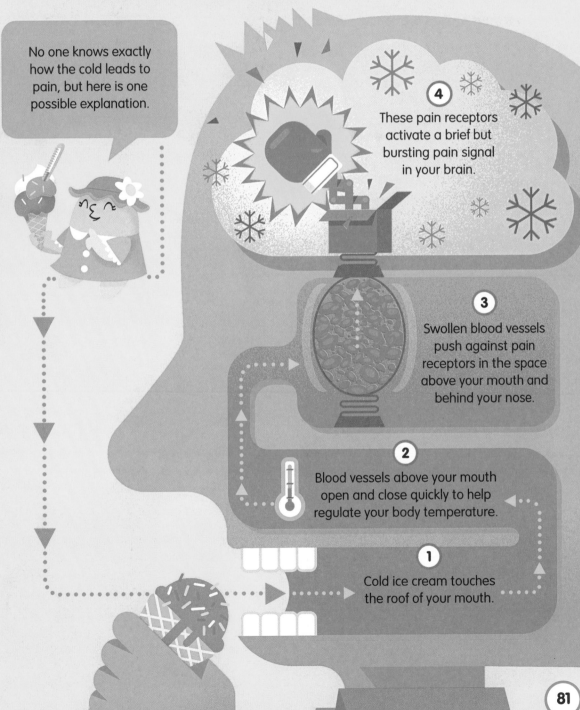

No one knows exactly how the cold leads to pain, but here is one possible explanation.

4 These pain receptors activate a brief but bursting pain signal in your brain.

3 Swollen blood vessels push against pain receptors in the space above your mouth and behind your nose.

2 Blood vessels above your mouth open and close quickly to help regulate your body temperature.

1 Cold ice cream touches the roof of your mouth.

68 Some people can taste words...

or smell numbers.

In most people's brains, a sound is interpreted simply as a sound. But for some people, a sound creates a noise *and* another sensation too, such as taste or smell. This kind of experience – when one sense becomes two – is known as **synesthesia**.

How your brain experiences sound

1

Air vibrates and goes into your ear.

2
Sense receptors in your ear turn vibrations into electrical signals.

3
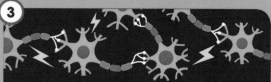
The signals are passed into and through your brain along a network of cells called **neurons**.

4
The movement of signals along a particular network creates the sensation of hearing a sound.

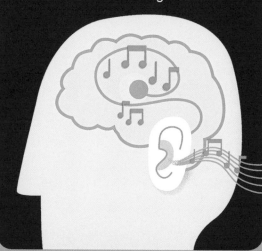

How synesthesia happens

1
Sense receptors turn vibrations into electrical signals...

2
...but the signals pass along many more neurons, and sometimes along multiple networks.

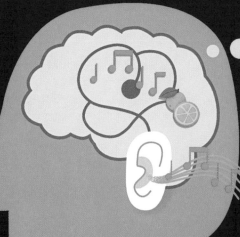

3

The mixture of networks creates the sensation of sound but also of a particular taste, or smell, or sight.

82

Every person with **synesthesia** has a different experience.

Names with an 'mmm' sound are yellow.

Numbers with a '7' in them smell of oranges.

17

Amy

The symbol **%** tastes like jelly.

No it doesn't! It tastes like **chalk**.

25% OFF

No one knows why some brains are like this, but it affects roughly 1 in every 200 people.

69 Your body could be an illusion...

and your brain would never know.

Your brain uses your senses to confirm details about what it expects to see and hear around you. If someone fed false information to your brain, it wouldn't know the difference between reality and illusion.

It's possible to send signals directly into the brain that *mimic* sensations such as light, sounds, touch and so on.

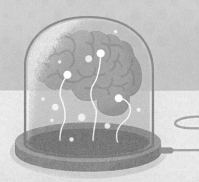

In fact, your brain could be wired to a computer controlled by aliens, and you'd have no way to know for sure.

70 A single head of hair...

could support a small army.

Hair is soft to touch and can bend in any direction, yet it is incredibly strong.
The secret to its strength is its structure, and the tough protein chain inside.

**Inside a strand
of hair**

Hair is made
up of lots of
tiny cables...

...that contain
even tinier cables...

A full head of hair, on average, has around **100,000 strands**.

Altogether, that means a whole head of hair could support around **10 tons** – the weight of around 100 knights in armor.

...that hide tinier cables still.

They are made of a protein called **keratin**, which forms tough, twisted chains that are tightly bound together.

Keratin can stretch and bend like a spring without breaking.

A single strand of hair can support **3.5 ounces** – the weight of a bar of soap.

71 Deliberately infecting yourself...

can stop you from getting sick in the future.

A treatment called **inoculation** makes your body resist particular diseases. It works by infecting you with a weak version of a germ, so your body knows what to expect if you come into contact with it for real later on.

An inoculation puts a small dose of **antigens** from a specific disease into your body.

HERE WE GO.

Your immune system creates **antibodies** that destroy those antigens.

TAKE THAT!

From then on, your body remembers how to make these antibodies...

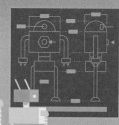

...and keeps lots of them on standby too.

If you come into contact with the disease naturally in the future, your body can fight off the antigens so quickly that you don't get sick. This is known as **immunity**.

UH-OH, WE'RE DONE FOR!

72 A deadly disease was destroyed...

thanks to milkmaids.

Smallpox was a terrible disease that caused painful skin sores and killed millions of people. At first, inoculations were risky and many patients died, but eventually a safe treatment was discovered and the disease was wiped out.

1000s
The first inoculations happened in China. Scabs were used to transfer the disease, but often the dose was too strong and patients became ill.

1720s
English traveler **Lady Mary Montagu** witnessed an inoculation in Turkey. Back home, she told everyone what she had learned.

1770s
Dr. Edward Jenner heard that milkmaids rarely caught smallpox. The reason was that they had already caught a similar but milder disease called **cowpox**, from the cows they milked.

1790s
Jenner developed a cowpox inoculation that also prevented smallpox. It worked because cowpox antigens are very similar to smallpox ones.

Jenner called his treatment **vaccination**, after the Latin word for cow – *vacca*.

Smallpox Died 1980

Vaccinations were given all over the world, and smallpox was eventually wiped out.

73 Your body was a tube...

for the first ten days.

You began your life as a tiny ball called an **embryo**. When you were growing in your mother's womb, the first shape you took was a tube with holes at either end. The rest of your body soon followed.

Your body started as a tiny ball-shaped blob...

Embryo

Then it became a tube...

This tube became your **digestive system**...

...forming holes at both ends.

The rest of your body developed around the tube:

Your **brain** was the first organ to develop.

Then your **heart** started beating...

...and your **eyes** began to form.

After just 8 weeks, you looked recognizably human.

Your **fingernails, toenails** and **nose** took shape.

Embryo	Tube	Mouth	Brain	Heart	Eyes		Nails	Nose
3 days	*5 days*	*10 days*	*18 days*	*3 weeks*	*4 weeks*		*10 weeks*	*11 weeks*

74 You were an apple...

before you were a mango.

To help pregnant mothers visualize how their babies are growing, many doctors describe their size by comparing them to fruits.

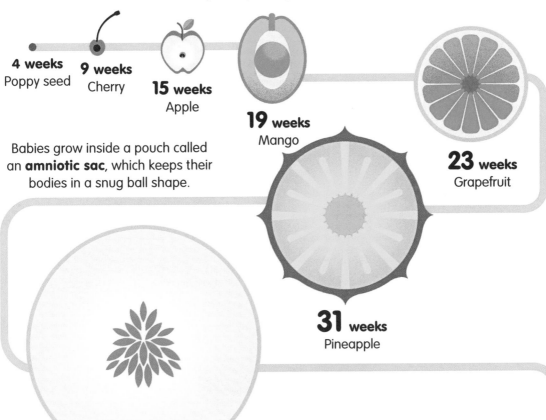

4 weeks
Poppy seed

9 weeks
Cherry

15 weeks
Apple

19 weeks
Mango

23 weeks
Grapefruit

Babies grow inside a pouch called an **amniotic sac**, which keeps their bodies in a snug ball shape.

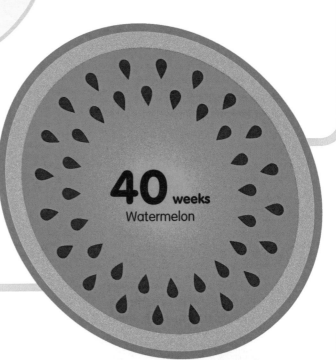

31 weeks
Pineapple

36 weeks
Honeydew melon

40 weeks
Watermelon

Most babies are ready to be born after about 40 weeks. Some can be as big as a watermelon, but are usually half as heavy.

75 Learning to sew...

is part of a doctor's training.

Doctors usually close up cuts or wounds by sewing the skin edges together. This helps the wound form a seal so it can heal naturally.

Surgeons use a special needle and thread to close up the skin. They use a variety of different stitches, depending on the type of wound, then secure the stiches with a knot.

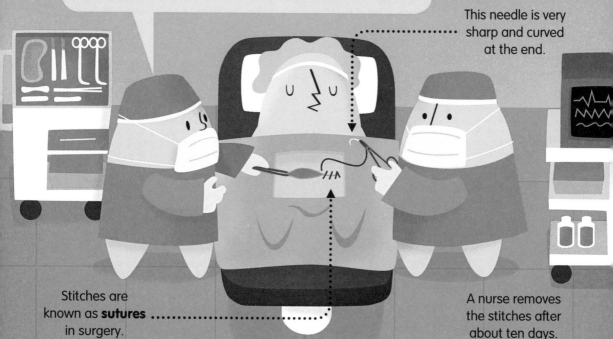

This needle is very sharp and curved at the end.

Stitches are known as **sutures** in surgery.

A nurse removes the stitches after about ten days.

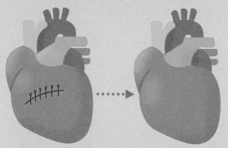

To close wounds deep under the skin, doctors can use dissolvable stitches that don't need to be removed at a later date.

Dissolvable stitches start to break down naturally as the wound heals. After a few weeks, they disappear completely.

Other methods of closing wounds

Staples

Often used for speed and to close head wounds

Tape

Used for minor wounds

Glue

Minor cuts with straight edges

In the 19th century, German doctor Adolph Kussmaul visited a famous sword swallower.

How does he do it?

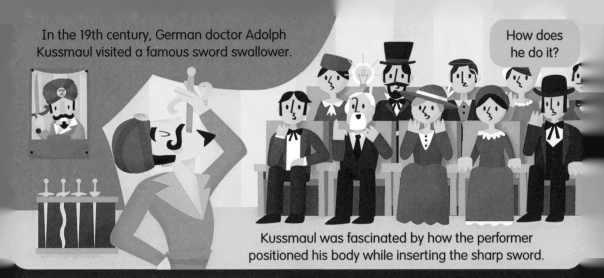

Kussmaul was fascinated by how the performer positioned his body while inserting the sharp sword.

Inspired by this act, Kussmaul made an **endoscope** – a brass tube for looking into patients' throats and stomachs.

Kussmaul's tube was long and rigid, and awkward to use.

Ow!

So in 1868 Kussmaul hired the sword swallower to show off his new invention.

This led to the invention of flexible endoscopes – attached to video cameras – in the 1950s.

So now doctors *and* patients can see inside their stomachs.

77 If a man never shaved...

his beard would grow twice as long as his body.

Men's beards start growing when they become teenagers. Like the hair on their heads, beards keep growing. If a man never shaved, his beard could be over 12ft long by the time he reached 70.

The longest beard in recorded history measured

17ft, 6in.

It was grown by Norwegian-American farmer Hans Langseth, who died at age 81 in 1927.

To stop it from breaking, he braided the lower part and carried it in a **pouch**.

Mustache

Chin curtain

The oldest known razors, made from sharpened flint, were invented at least

30,000 years ago.

Ever since, men all over the world have created many different styles of facial hair.

Goatee

Van Dyke

Full beard

Soul patch

Sideburns

Mutton chops

Scary movies...

really can get under your skin.

Human bodies are designed to react to stressful situations. When you watch a suspenseful, tense or scary sequence in a movie, your *mind* knows it's not really happening. But your *body*, especially your hormones, can react as if you're really in the middle of it...

Effects inside your body while you watch

You feel tense, as your body is flooded with adrenaline...

...as well as pain-suppressing hormones.

Your heart beats faster, pumping blood around at great speed.

Inside your blood, you make extra platelets to help cuts heal...

...and extra white blood cells, to help fight off infections.

As blood flows faster, it can make your skin feel hotter, and your core feel colder.

Hours, and even days, after you've finished the movie, you can experience interrupted sleep patterns and nightmares.

People don't all find the same things scary. So these reactions don't happen to everyone every time they watch a movie.

79 Stones in your ears...

help you stay on your feet.

Deep inside your ears are tiny stones called **otoliths**. As you move, these stones are pushed and pulled up, down or sideways. The way they move tells your brain which way up your head is, helping you to balance.

1

Otoliths are contained in tiny pouches, called the **utricle** and the **saccule**, in each ear.

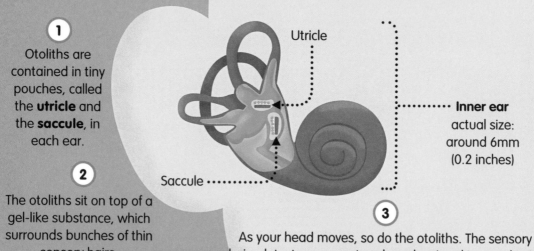

Utricle

Inner ear
actual size:
around 6mm
(0.2 inches)

Saccule

2

The otoliths sit on top of a gel-like substance, which surrounds bunches of thin sensory hairs.

3

As your head moves, so do the otoliths. The sensory hairs detect movement and send a signal to your brain.

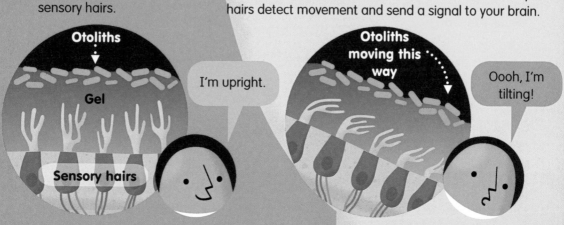

Otoliths

Gel

Sensory hairs

I'm upright.

Otoliths moving this way

Oooh, I'm tilting!

Sometimes, otoliths can fall out of place, causing a condition known as **vertigo**. This can make people feel dizzy, even if they aren't moving very much.

Luckily, there's a way to get stones back into position: wiggle a patient's head around, following a sequence known as the **Epley Maneuver**.

80 Babies see red...

before they see blue.

Although most babies are born with color sensors in their eyes, it can take several weeks before they learn how to use them. Nearly all babies learn to see shades of red first, and shades of blue last.

For the first few days, babies see blurry images only.

After a week or two, most can focus on shapes and patterns, and can recognize faces.

They can start to see red any time between one week and three months old.

Most babies can see all colors by the time they're six months old, and some much sooner than that.

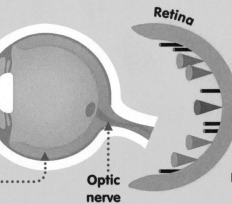

How eyes see shape and color

Retina

Pupil – light enters the eye here

Retina – where light is processed by two types of cells, called **cones** and **rods**.

Optic nerve

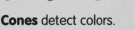
Rods help the eye to pick out shapes, and different shades of black, white and gray.

Cones detect colors. Different cones are sensitive to different colors.

81 Identical twins...

are up to 10 times rarer than non-identical twins.

Around the world, between 10 and 30 out of every 1,000 births result in twin babies. But only 3 in 1,000 births result in identical twin babies.

How non-identical twins happen

Two babies form side by side, in two separate blobs called **zygotes**...

...that will grow into bigger blobs called **embryos**.

These gradually grow into babies, known technically as **dyzygotic** twins.

> Non-identical twins are no more alike than brothers and sisters born through separate pregnancies.

How identical twins happen

A single zygote forms in its mother's womb.

After a few days, the zygote splits in two, and forms two identical embryos.

> Identical twins share the same DNA, which means they usually grow up to look very similar, and even behave in similar ways.

These will grow into identical twins, known technically as **monozygotic twins**.

82 Children born years apart...

could still be twins.

Most twins grow together in their mother's womb, and are born on the same day. But dyzygotic twins (or triplets, quadruplets and more) can be *conceived* on the same day, but *born* at different times.

1 Doctors can create lots of zygotes all at once, using a technique called *in vitro fertilization*, or **IVF**.

In vitro means 'in glass' in Latin.

These zygotes are twins, although they're not identical twins.

2

In a lab, the zygotes grow into embryos.

3

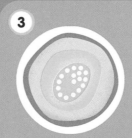

A doctor places one embryo in a woman's womb...

...where it grows into a baby.

4

The twin – and any other embryos – can be stored safely, in a freezer, for years.

5 Some years later, the doctor places the second embryo into its mother's womb, where it grows into a baby.

Look, it's my new baby twin sister!

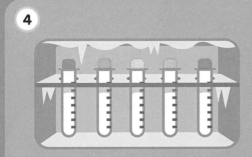

83 You don't need your spleen...

but it helps.

Your body is designed to work with all of its organs intact. But you can still survive without some organs entirely, and without large portions of others.

Brain
You can survive with only half, either right or left.

Lungs
You can survive with just one.

Liver
You can lose up to 60%, which will grow back.

Spleen
You don't *need* it, but it helps the body fight off infections.

Stomach and **small intestine**
You can live without one or the other or parts of both.

Kidneys
You can survive with just one, or even *none*, with the help of a machine.

Gallbladder and **pancreas**
If these stop working, you can take supplements of the enzymes they make.

Large intestine
Most of this, including your colon, can be replaced with a bag.

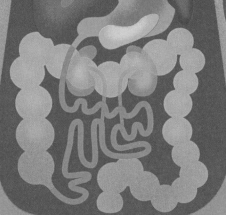

84 Pain-free surgery...

was discovered by accident.

Drugs that can stop people from feeling pain during surgery are known as **anesthetics**. One of the first to be used was a gas called **nitrous oxide** – also known as **laughing gas**. It took four different people to turn the gas from an accidental discovery into a medical invention.

1772
Nitrous oxide gas was first discovered by **Joseph Priestley**.

1794
James Watt invented a way to trap gases, and a way for people to inhale them, using a kind of balloon.

1798
Humphry Davy tested nitrous oxide on himself. It made him light-headed and happy. He thought it might be useful for doctors...

...but instead, foolish young rich people inhaled it at dangerous 'laughing gas parties'.

1844
Dentist **Horace Wells** volunteered to test nitrous oxide in a surgical procedure.

He reported feeling no pain while a fellow dentist extracted one of his teeth.

21st century

Nitrous oxide is still used in some countries today to help ease pain in the early stages of childbirth.

85 Medieval medicine...

still has a lot to teach us.

Researchers around the world still read through ancient medical text books to learn about remedies, and test them in modern scientific conditions. A treatment for eye infections, found in an Anglo-Saxon work called *Bald's Leechbook*, turned out to be successful in a 2015 experiment.

Take a portion of leeks...

an equal measure of garlic...

bile from a young bull...

...and a splash of wine.

Keep it in a brass vessel for nine days.

In 2015, researchers followed the **9th-century recipe** as closely as they could. They found it really did help fight off bacteria that cause *styes*, painful swellings on eyelids.

They're now investigating which part of the recipe is effective, with the hope of creating a new medicine.

86 A medical mystery...

was solved with a map.

In the 1850s, people thought diseases such as **cholera** were spread through the air in a kind of mist. But a doctor named John Snow used a map of London to show that cholera spread through filthy water.

In 1854, there was a sudden outbreak of cholera in London's Soho. About 500 people died in ten days.

Snow marked each death on a map. He also marked the positions of water pumps, which provided water to local residents.

His map showed a high number of deaths occurred near one particular water pump on Broad Street.

Soho, London

— one cholera death

💧 water pump

Deadly water pump

BROAD STREET
(now Broadwick Street)

MARSHALL STREET

CARNABY STREET

BERWICK STREET

SILVER STREET

GREAT PULTENEY STREET

BREWER STREET

GOLDEN SQUARE

At Snow's insistence, the pump was closed. Sure enough, the cholera outbreak quickly subsided.

Doctors still use maps today to find out where outbreaks of diseases start from.

How much it hurts...

depends on where it hurts.

Receptors in your skin tell the brain what you're touching. Some parts of your body have far more than others, which makes them more sensitive to touch.

This is an imaginary figure called a **cortical homunculus**. It shows what a person would look like if each body part was in proportion to the number of touch receptors it had – the more sensitive the area, the bigger it appears.

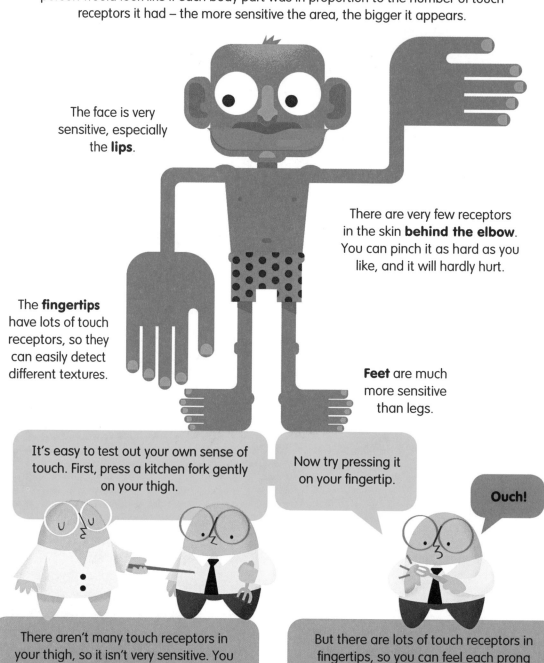

The face is very sensitive, especially the **lips**.

There are very few receptors in the skin **behind the elbow**. You can pinch it as hard as you like, and it will hardly hurt.

The **fingertips** have lots of touch receptors, so they can easily detect different textures.

Feet are much more sensitive than legs.

It's easy to test out your own sense of touch. First, press a kitchen fork gently on your thigh.

Now try pressing it on your fingertip.

Ouch!

There aren't many touch receptors in your thigh, so it isn't very sensitive. You can't even feel the individual prongs.

But there are lots of touch receptors in fingertips, so you can feel each prong individually – and it hurts much more.

88 Brains don't feel pain...

so patients can be kept awake during brain surgery.

During most operations, patients are put to sleep to stop them from feeling pain. However, the brain doesn't contain any pain receptors, so once the surgeon has opened the skull, the patient is often woken up and spoken to.

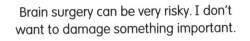

89 Recycling blood...

keeps you alive.

Your two kidneys perform a life-saving job: filtering blood to remove waste. They recycle the rest of the blood and make sure it contains the correct ingredients to keep all the other parts of your body working.

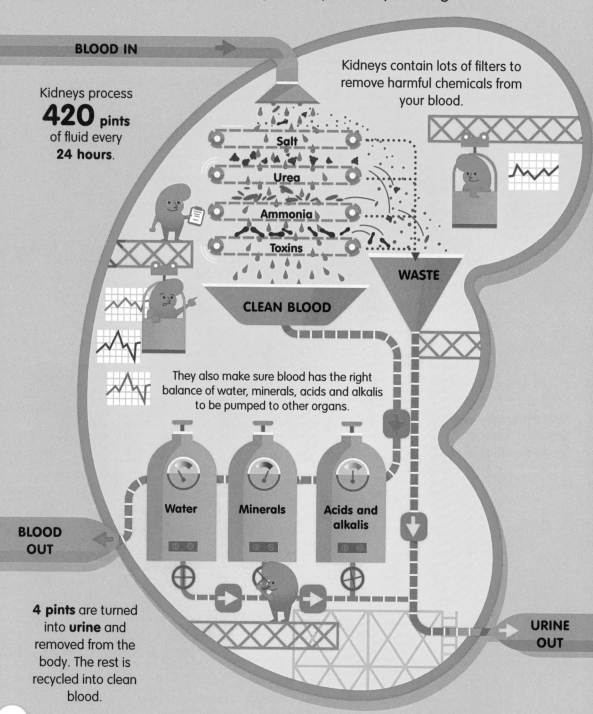

BLOOD IN

Kidneys process **420** pints of fluid every **24 hours**.

Kidneys contain lots of filters to remove harmful chemicals from your blood.

Salt

Urea

Ammonia

Toxins

WASTE

CLEAN BLOOD

They also make sure blood has the right balance of water, minerals, acids and alkalis to be pumped to other organs.

Water

Minerals

Acids and alkalis

BLOOD OUT

4 pints are turned into **urine** and removed from the body. The rest is recycled into clean blood.

URINE OUT

90 More than half your bones...

are in your hands and feet.

An adult human hand is made of 27 bones, and a foot is made of 26.
That's a total of 106 bones to make two hands and two feet.

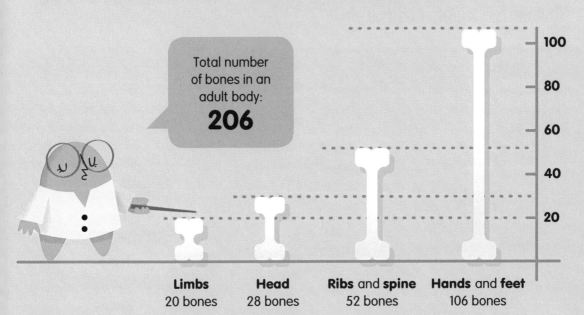

Total number of bones in an adult body:
206

Limbs	Head	Ribs and spine	Hands and feet
20 bones	28 bones	52 bones	106 bones

100
80
60
40
20

BUILD YOUR OWN

HUMAN HAND

You will need:

Distal phalanges x 5 ···▶

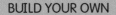 ◀··· Middle phalanges x 4

Proximal phalanges x 5 ···▶

◀··· Metacarpals x 5

Carpals x 8 ···▶

JUST ADD MUSCLES...

...to this exquisitely designed tool, and you can stretch, twist, bend, grip and squeeze!

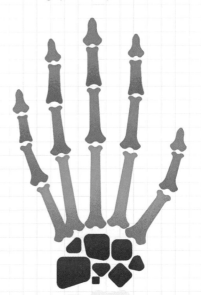

91 3-D printers...

can build living body parts.

3-D printers usually print plastic and metal objects. But scientists are developing 3-D printers that print soft, jello-like shapes containing cartilage made from human cells.

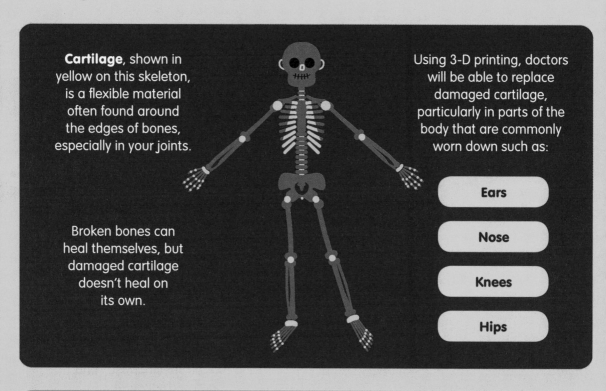

Cartilage, shown in yellow on this skeleton, is a flexible material often found around the edges of bones, especially in your joints.

Broken bones can heal themselves, but damaged cartilage doesn't heal on its own.

Using 3-D printing, doctors will be able to replace damaged cartilage, particularly in parts of the body that are commonly worn down such as:

Ears

Nose

Knees

Hips

Here's how 3-D printing could help to rebuild a patient's nose:

A doctor extracts cartilage cells from the patient, then mixes them with a liquid gel.

The printer builds a 3-D gel nose in layers. This takes about 20 minutes.

A surgeon **implants** or places the nose on the patient in surgery.

The new nose grows naturally because it contains some of the patient's own cells.

92 Even if you're a good liar...
your body might give you away.

A **polygraph**, or lie detector, is a machine that monitors how your body reacts when you answer a question. By tracking four key indicators, it can tell the difference between when you're telling the truth and when you're telling a lie.

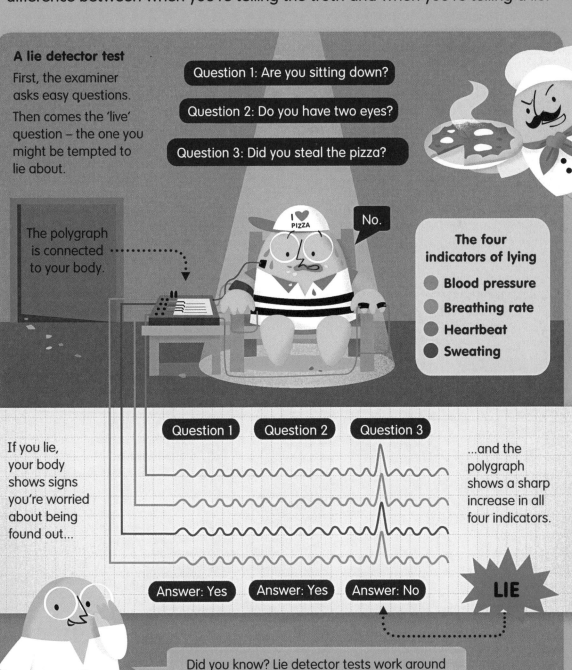

A lie detector test

First, the examiner asks easy questions.

Then comes the 'live' question – the one you might be tempted to lie about.

Question 1: Are you sitting down?

Question 2: Do you have two eyes?

Question 3: Did you steal the pizza?

No.

The polygraph is connected to your body.

The four indicators of lying

- Blood pressure
- Breathing rate
- Heartbeat
- Sweating

If you lie, your body shows signs you're worried about being found out...

Question 1   Question 2   Question 3

...and the polygraph shows a sharp increase in all four indicators.

Answer: Yes   Answer: Yes   Answer: No

LIE

Did you know? Lie detector tests work around 4 out of 5 times. Some people can control their bodies, stopping the indicators from changing.

93 You have more than five senses...

in fact you might have more than twenty.

For thousands of years, scientists and philosophers have debated exactly what counts as a sense. Traditionally, people talk about the five senses of **touch**, **sight**, **taste**, **hearing** and **smell** – but by most modern reckonings, there are many more than this.

Senses are your body's way of perceiving the world. Here are the five traditional senses and some others that are less obvious.

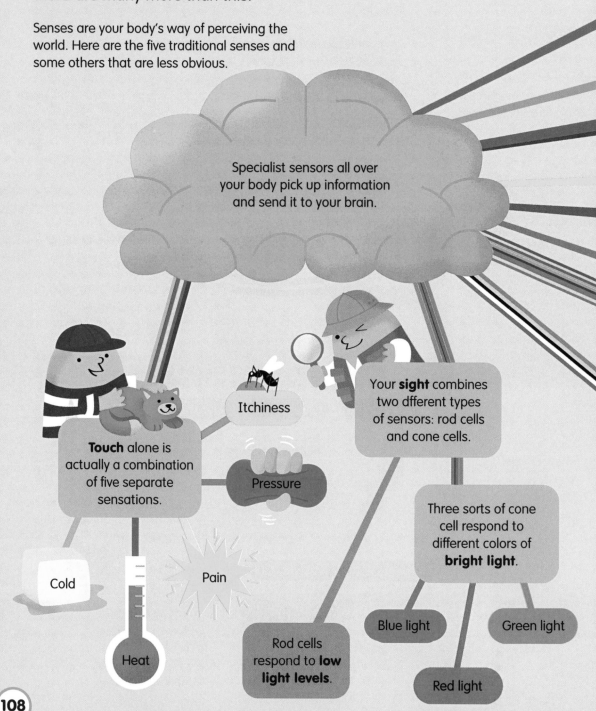

Specialist sensors all over your body pick up information and send it to your brain.

Itchiness

Your **sight** combines two dfferent types of sensors: rod cells and cone cells.

Touch alone is actually a combination of five separate sensations.

Pressure

Three sorts of cone cell respond to different colors of **bright light**.

Cold

Pain

Blue light

Green light

Heat

Rod cells respond to **low light levels**.

Red light

Chemical sensors in your blood check your glucose levels. This creates a sense of **hunger**.

Other sensors check salt levels in your blood. This sets off your sense of **thirst**.

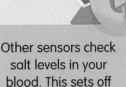

Sensors in your **bladder** and **bowels** let your body know when it's time to use the toilet.

There is a sense that allows you to touch your fingertips without looking. This is known as **proprioception**. It tells you where your muscles and limbs are in relation to each other.

The movement of fluid and stones in your inner ear gives you a sense of **balance**.

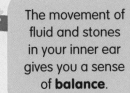

Sensors in your ears respond to vibrating soundwaves to give you a sense of **hearing**.

Hundreds of different chemical sensors in your nose target the molecules that you inhale to give you a sense of **smell**.

At least five distinct sensations in your mouth combine to create **taste**.

Sweet

Sour

Bitter

Salty

Umami

Umami is a savory taste found in meat and tomatoes.

Your senses of taste and smell work together to help you perceive **flavor**.

94 You grow a new liver...

every single year.

Your body is made up of cells that are constantly dying. But in most parts, new ones grow in their place. In this way, your body is gradually renewed, piece by piece, over and over again.

Here's how long cells in different parts of the body last before they are renewed:

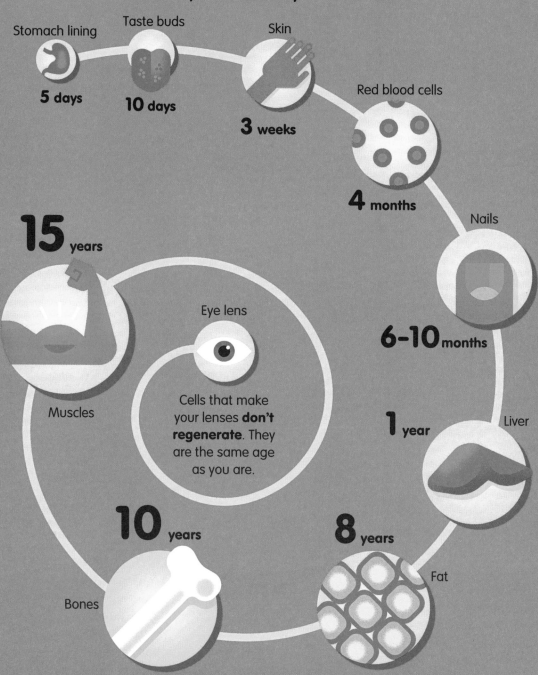

Stomach lining
5 days

Taste buds
10 days

Skin
3 weeks

Red blood cells
4 months

Nails
6-10 months

Liver
1 year

Fat
8 years

Bones
10 years

Muscles
15 years

Eye lens
Cells that make your lenses **don't regenerate**. They are the same age as you are.

95 21st-century surgeons...

still use Stone-Age tools.

Prehistoric people made cutting tools from an incredibly sharp material called **obsidian** – a black glass formed by volcanoes. Today, some surgeons use scalpels made from obsidian, rather than metal blades.

Skip Ad ▶️

STEEL BLADE

OBSIDIAN BLADE

Seen under a microscope, sharpened **steel blades** are actually jagged.

BUY NOW!

Sharpened **obsidian blades** have smooth, clean edges – even under a microscope.

Obsidian scalpels leave smaller scars that can heal much faster than scars made by metal scalpels.

96 Babies grow mustaches...

while they are still in the womb.

About four months into its life, a baby in the womb starts to grow hair, called **lanugo**, over most of its body. It grows first on the upper lip.

Lanugo usually drops off before the baby is born...

...and the baby swallows the hairs.

What doesn't kill bacteria...

can make them stronger.

Drugs known as **antibiotics** can cure diseases caused by tiny creatures called **bacteria**. Antibiotics work by killing off the bad bacteria in a person's body. But they don't always kill *all* the bad bacteria. The toughest can survive...

Some kinds of bacteria can make you unwell.

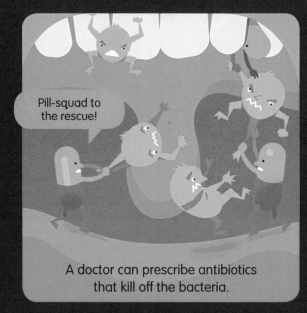

A doctor can prescribe antibiotics that kill off the bacteria.

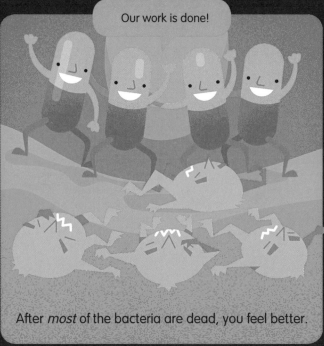

After *most* of the bacteria are dead, you feel better.

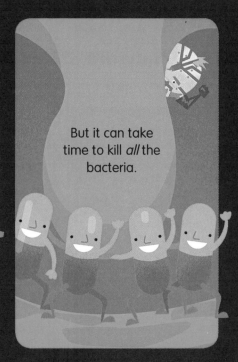

Sometimes, new bacteria can appear that are super tough.

Puny pills can't hurt me!

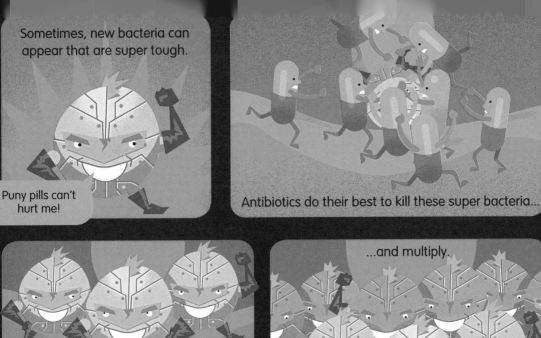

Antibiotics do their best to kill these super bacteria...

...and multiply.

...but some of them may survive, and start to multiply...

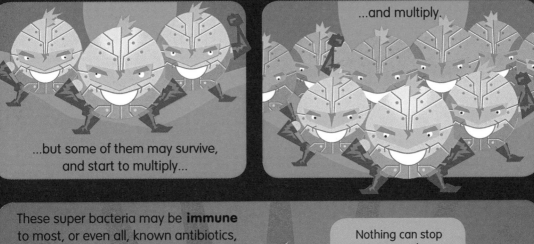

These super bacteria may be **immune** to most, or even all, known antibiotics, and can cause deadly infections.

Nothing can stop us now!

Sometimes, people take antibiotics to fight infections caused by **viruses**.

But antibiotics have **no effect** on viruses, or the symptoms of the illnesses they cause.

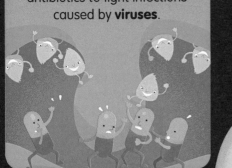

Using antibiotics makes it easier for new super bacteria to appear, so it's very important to only take them when you absolutely need to.

98 The best way to learn...

is to fall asleep.

One of the most important things your brain does when you're asleep is remind itself about things you've learned during the day. This includes practical skills, such as music and sports, as well as filing away new facts.

Experts describe four stages, known as a **sleep cycle**. In a good night's sleep, most people complete 4 or 5 cycles.

1

Light sleep

Eyes closed; brain activity slows down

Muscles start to relax, but can sometimes twitch, waking a person up.

2

Main sleep

Body and brain at their least active

A few people experience sleepwalking or sleeptalking during this stage.

It's easy to wake up during stages 1 and 4, but very hard during stages 2 and 3.

Dreaming permits each and every one of us to be quietly and safely insane every night of our lives.
– Professor William Dement, founder of the American Academy of Sleep Medicine

4

REM sleep
(short for Rapid Eye Movement)

Eyes move rapidly, heart beats faster, breathing rate goes up; skeletal muscles don't move; brain very active

Dreaming occurs – but no one knows how it happens or what it is for.

3

Slow-wave sleep

Brain files away memories

The body can repair itself by building new cells rapidly.

You can improve your health, your ability to do sports and your ability to learn by making sure you get enough sleep.

99 Everybody hiccups...

but no one knows why.

When you hiccup, the muscles that help you breathe suddenly contract, and your vocal cords snap shut. This causes the characteristic jerk and sound of a hiccup. Although scientists know *how* we hiccup, they still don't know why.

Some scientists have a theory that hiccups serve a useful purpose early on in life:

hic

hic

1

They might help us learn to breathe in the womb.

2

They might help babies clear air from their stomach, so they can drink more milk.

Other scientists think hiccups aren't useful at all – they're just a feature left over from prehistoric times.

hic

As well as not knowing why we hiccup, scientists still don't know a reliable way to stop them when they've started.

100 Breathe a sigh of relief...
it keeps your lungs from collapsing.

Extra deep breaths, or **sighs**, often express emotions such as sadness or relief. They also play another, less obvious role, which is vital to keeping you alive: preventing tiny air sacs in your lungs from collapsing.

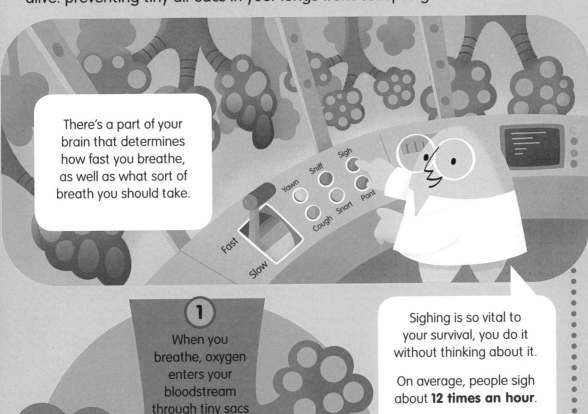

There's a part of your brain that determines how fast you breathe, as well as what sort of breath you should take.

Yawn Sniff Sigh
Cough Snort Pant

Fast

Slow

1 When you breathe, oxygen enters your bloodstream through tiny sacs in your lungs called **alveoli**.

2 Over time, your alveoli can collapse...

3 ...which could lead to lung failure.

4 Sighing keeps this in check by reinflating collapsed alveoli.

Sighing is so vital to your survival, you do it without thinking about it.

On average, people sigh about **12 times an hour**.

Sigh...

Collapsed alveoli

Normal alveoli

Major organs and glands

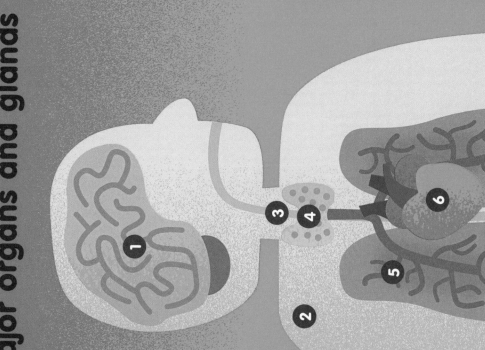

Major bones

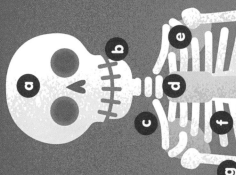

a skull	**h** radius	**o** femur	
b mandible	**i** ulna	**p** patella	
c clavicle	**j** spine	**q** tibia	
d sternum	**k** pelvis	**r** fibula	
e scapula	**l** carpals	**s** tarsals	
f ribcage	**m** metacarpals	**t** metatarsals	
g humerus	**n** phalanges (hand)	**u** phalanges (foot)	

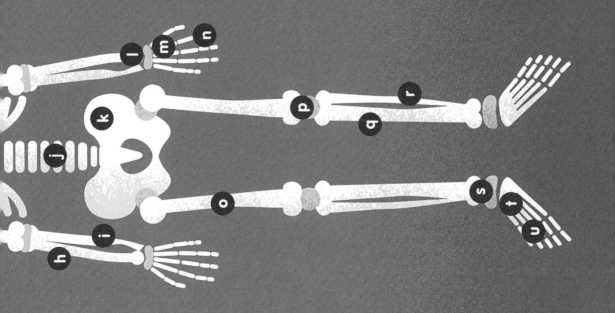

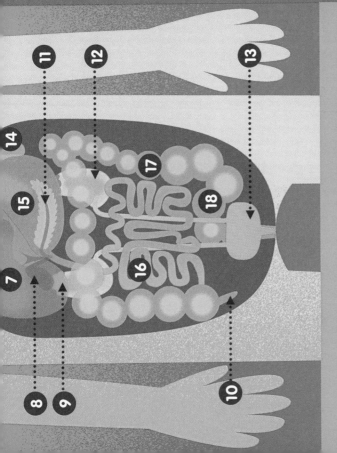

1 brain
2 skin
3 esophagus
4 thyroid
5 lung
6 heart
7 liver
8 gallbladder
9 adrenal gland
10 appendix
11 pancreas
12 kidney
13 bladder
14 spleen
15 stomach
16 small intestine
17 large intestine
18 rectum

Glossary

This glossary explains some of the words used in this book, as well as some of the words doctors often use to refer to different parts of the body. Words written in *italic* type have their own entries. You can find a list of medical professions on page 123.

abdominal To do with the part of your body containing the digestive and reproductive organs.

anesthetic A substance that can temporarily stop your body, or part of your body, from feeling any pain.

antibiotic A type of *medicine* that can kill *bacteria*. Antibiotics do not have any effect on *viruses*.

antibody A type of *protein* made in your blood that can attack and destroy a specific *antigen*. Antibodies are part of your *immune system*.

antigen Part of a *germ*, or other substance, that can be recognized and attacked by your *immune system*.

aural To do with your ears or hearing.

axillary To do with your armpits.

bacteria Tiny creatures that can live inside people, or pass from one person to another. Most bacteria are harmless, or even helpful. Some cause diseases.

blood pressure The force with which your blood flows. If your blood pressure is very high or very low, it can be a sign that you are unwell.

bronchial To do with the airways in your lungs.

cardiac To do with your heart.

cartilage Soft, flexible bone-like *tissue* that covers some parts of your bones.

cell One of trillions of tiny building blocks that make up almost every part of your body. Most cells contain *DNA*.

cerebral To do with your brain.

cholangio To do with your bile duct.

colonic To do with your large intestine.

costal To do with your ribs.

cranial To do with your head.

diagnosis A decision by a medical professional about the cause of your particular **symptoms**.

digestive system The name for the series of parts of your body that help to process food and drink.

digital To do with your fingers or toes.

DNA The chemical code that tells your body how to build itself. Parents pass their DNA on to their children.

drug Any *medicine* or other substance that affects a person's body, usually through the blood. Most drugs are designed to help fight back against an illness, but some can affect people's mood and behavior, too.

element The basic chemical substances that act as the building blocks of all the substances on Earth.

embryo The name for the small collection of *cells* that can grow into a baby.

endocrine To do with the glands that produce your hormones.

enteric To do with your gut.

epidermal To do with your outer skin.

gastric To do with your stomach.

gene A section of *DNA* that provides the code for how your body is built.

germs The name for tiny creatures that can attack your body, often causing illness. Germs include *bacteria* and *viruses*.

gland A small *organ*, or part of an organ, that releases *hormones*.

gut The long tube that forms the main part of your *digestive system*, starting at your mouth and ending at your anus.

hepatic To do with your liver.

hormone A chemical released from your *glands* into your blood to send signals to other parts of your body.

immune system Your body's own defence mechanism, that works by creating *cells* and chemicals that can identify and destroy *germs*.

immunity If your body is able to fight off the *germs* that cause a disease before you suffer any *symptoms*, you have an *immunity* to that disease.

inoculation Deliberately infecting someone with a small dose of a *virus* to help your body develop an *immunity* to that virus.

mandibular To do with your lower jaw.

medicine A *drug* that helps a person fight off an illness, or manage a condition.

nasal To do with your nose.

nervous system Your brain and spinal cord and the network of nerve cells that carry messages to and from your whole body.

neuron The scientific name for a nerve *cell*.

nutrients The parts of food and drink, such as vitamins, minerals and proteins, that your body needs to stay healthy.

operation Any medical procedure in which a *surgeon* cuts into a person's body.

ophthalmic or **optic** To do with your eyes.

oral To do with your mouth.

orbital To do with your eye sockets.

organ A particular part of your body, usually soft, that carries out a particular set of jobs. See page 118 for a list of organs.

osteo To do with your bones.

oxygen A gas that your body needs to survive. You breathe it in from the air, and it is carried in your blood.

pore A small opening in your skin, that lets your body sweat.

protein A type of substance that makes up most parts of your body, such as muscles.

pulmonary – to do with your lungs

pulse The rhythmic throbbing of arteries as they carry blood around the body. You can feel your pulse in your wrist or neck.

receptor The end of a nerve cell that reacts to sensations by sending a message to your brain through your *nervous system*.

regeneration Your body's ability to grow back certain parts, especially cells.

renal To do with your kidneys.

scalp The skin on your head.

scalpel A knife with a small, very sharp blade. *Surgeons* often use scalpels to cut into a person's body during an *operation*.

sense The ways that your body perceives what is going on in the world outside, for example by seeing or hearing, and the ways your body finds out about itself, for example hunger and thirst.

symptom A sign or indication in your body, such as pain or unusual tiredness, that you notice when you are unwell.

tissue The stuff your body is made of, such as *bone tissue* or *muscle tissue*.

thoracic To do with your upper chest.

urine The scientific word for wee – a mixture of water and waste substances filtered out of your blood by your kidneys.

virus An incredibly tiny creature, smaller than a *cell*, that can infect your body and make you unwell.

womb An *organ* in a woman's body where an *embryo* can grow into a baby. Its scientific name is *uterus*.

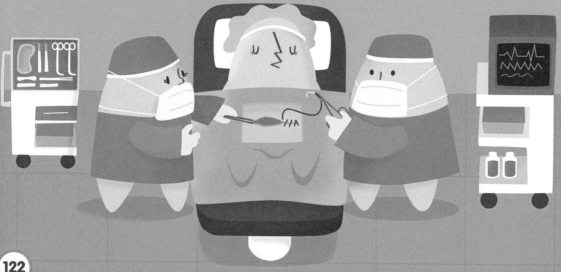

You don't have to be a doctor... to help treat people who are sick.

A doctor is a professional who is qualified and licensed to diagnose and treat people who are sick. Most specialize in specific areas – and lots of healthcare work is done by people who aren't doctors.

anesthetist A doctor who prepares patients for surgery by giving them *anesthetic* medication.

biomedical scientist A person trained to work in a hospital lab, examining *tissue* samples from patients.

dietitian An expert in human *nutrition* and diet, and conditions relating to them.

GP Short for **General Practitioner**, your family doctor. Your GP can make an initial *diagnosis* if you're unwell.

dentist A doctor who specializes in the health of teeth, gums, and the mouth.

midwife A person trained to look after women and babies during pregnancy and childbirth.

nurse A nurse works with doctors and other healthcare staff to look after patients in hospitals and many other places.

occupational therapist A person trained to help people overcome and live with phsyical disabilities.

pediatrician A doctor who specializes in children and their illnesses.

paramedic A person trained to provide first aid in an emergency situation outside a hospital, and to bring them to a hospital safely and quickly, often in an ambulance.

pathologist A doctor who specializes in understanding how diseases work, inclduing *diagnosing* what caused a person's death.

pharmacist A person trained to prepare and dispense medicines in a hospital or a pharmacy.

phlebotomist A person trained to take blood samples from people.

physician The general term for a doctor who studies, diagnoses and treats patients, often using medicines rather than surgery.

physiotherapist A person who is trained to help people recover from physical injuries or conditions affecting their ability to move.

psychiatrist A doctor who specializes in diseases and conditions that affect the mind.

psychologist A person who studies the way people think and behave; often someone who helps people identify and manage mental conditions.

radiographer A person trained to perform X-rays and scans that help *diagnose* diseases or other internal problems.

surgeon A doctor who performs *operations*.

Index

G

gallbladder, 98
gas, 15
gastric folds, 12
genes, 16
germs, 20, 44
glands, 8, 30, 59
glucose, 46
gluteus maximus, 26
gold, 29, 39
goosebumps, 11
Grandin, Temple, 58

H

hair, 5, 52, 66, 77,
   84-85, 111
hallucinations, 38, 72
hands, 70, 74, 105
hearing, 83, 108, 109
heart, 4, 8, 10, 31, 48-49, 63,
   67, 71, 80, 88
heartbeat, 31, 63, 93, 107, 115
height, 22, 76
herbal medicine, 19, 55
hiccups, 116
Hippocrates, 61
hormones, 8, 24, 30, 36, 42,
   53, 93
hug machine, 58
humours, 54-55
hunger, 109
hydrogen, 28

I

immune system, 9, 86, 112
inoculation, 86, 87
insulin, 46, 47
intervertebral discs, 22

intestines, 9, 62, 80
iron, 29
IVF (in vitro fertilization), 97

J

jaundice, 45
jaw, 26, 57, 65, 68
Jenner, Dr. Edward, 87

K

kidneys, 67, 71, 98, 104

L

lanugo, 111
large intestine, 13
lattimus dorsi, 26
laughing gas, 99
lead, 29
learning, 114-115
leukemia, 61
lie detectors, 107
lifetime, 4-5, 30, 68
lips, 103
liver, 45, 67, 98, 110
lungs, 4, 8, 10, 72-73, 78, 80,
   98, 117
lymph vessels, 9
lymphoma, 61

M

malaria, 19, 21
masseter, 26
medicines, 19, 47, 53, 54-55,
   99, 100, 101, 112-113
memory, 115
mercury, 29
metals, 12, 29

minerals, 104
Montagu, Lady Mary, 87
mouth, 14, 77, 81, 88
mucus, 12
muscles, 9, 10, 11, 14, 26-27,
   53, 67, 70, 110, 114, 116
muscular system, 9

N

nails, 5, 77, 88, 110
nerves, 7, 8, 53
nervous system, 8
neurons, 82
nitrogen, 28
noses, 5, 30, 64, 74, 77, 81,
   88, 106
nucleus, 16, 17, 28

O

oesophagus, 12
optical illusions, 50-51
organs, 9, 10, 98, 104
otoliths, 94
oxygen, 6, 8, 10, 28

P

pain, 7, 19, 36, 37, 71, 80, 99
pancreas, 46, 98
placebos, 53
plasma, 23
platelets, 23, 93
poison, 29
poo, 13
proprioception, 109
pulse rate, 32-33

Internet links

For links to websites where you can discover more surprising body facts, watch video clips and try quizzes and activities, go to the Usborne Quicklinks website at **www.usborne.com/quicklinks** and enter the keywords: **100 body things**.

Here are some of the things you can do at the websites we recommend:

• look at optical illusions that will baffle your brain
• follow a red blood cell around the human body
• see tiny dust mites that live on dead skin cells
• find out about many different parts of the brain, and learn what they can all do

The recommended websites are regularly reviewed and updated but, please note, Usborne Publishing is not responsible for the content of any website other than its own. We recommend that children are supervised while on the internet.

Usborne Publishing is not responsible and does not accept liability for the availability or content of any website other than its own, or for any exposure to harmful, offensive or inaccurate material which may appear on the Web. Usborne Publishing will have no liability for any damage or loss caused by viruses that may be downloaded as a result of browsing the sites it recommends.

Building a book...
needs a team of people with different skills.

Research and writing
Alex Frith
Minna Lacey
Jonathan Melmoth
Matthew Oldham
Darran Stobbart

Expert consultant
Dr. Kristina Routh

Series editor
Ruth Brocklehurst

American editor
Carrie Armstrong

Editorial director
Jane Chisholm

Layout and design
Matthew Bromley
Freya Harrison
Lenka Hrehova
Vickie Robinson

Illustration
Federico Mariani
Danny Schlitz

Series designer
Stephen Moncrieff

Art director
Mary Cartwright